LIGHT & Layered

KNITS

19 sophisticated designs
for every season

Vicki Square

INTERWEAVE
interweave.com

EDITOR Ann Budd
TECHNICAL EDITOR Eve Ng
CHARTS & SCHEMATICS Robyn Chachula
PHOTOGRAPHER Joe Hancock
PHOTO STYLIST Pamela Chavez
HAIR & MAKEUP Kathy MacKay
TEXT ILLUSTRATIONS Vicki Square
ART DIRECTOR Liz Quan
COVER & INTERIOR DESIGN Julia Boyles
PRODUCTION Katherine Jackson

Interweave Press LLC
A division of F+W Media Inc.
201 East Fourth Street
Loveland, CO 80537
interweave.com

Printed in China by Asia Pacific Offset Ltd.

Library of Congress
Cataloging-in-Publication Data

Square, Vicki, 1954-
  Light and layered knits : 19 sophisticated
designs for every season /
Vicki Square.
     pages cm
 ISBN 978-1-59668-795-0 (pbk.)
 ISBN 978-1-59668-894-0 (PDF)
1. Knitting--Patterns. I. Title.
 TT825.S7145 2013
 746.43'2041--dc23

2012033946
  5162 2560 6/13
10 9 8 7 6 5 4 3 2 1

ACKNOWLEDGMENTS

For Justine, the embodiment of class.

I am grateful to Interweave for being my long-time partner in creativity. I have much to be thankful for, including the many who have contributed to this book.

I thank Allison Korleski for her visionary look into this book's possibilities in the initial stages; Ann Budd for her attention to detail, her excellent editing skills, and her knowledgeable guidance; Eve Ng for her accurate technical editing and companionable way of working; Liz Quan for her complete understanding of my vision and her stylish art direction; Joe Hancock for his incredible artistry in photography, and his assistants, Jon Rose and Scott Wallace, for hospitality and fun; Kathy MacKay for lovely hair and makeup on models Ari, Christin, Eve, and Jessica, who brought my vision to life so beautifully; Pamela Chavez for providing just the right wardrobes; Julia Boyles for her graphic arts creativity in bringing a beautiful book to life; and Elisabeth Malzahn for expertly getting the word out. Finally, I thank Rebecca Campbell, whose constant encouragement, attention to schedule, and oversight kept me going with enthusiasm.

Honors go to my knitting family, who work tirelessly to help me achieve my goals. My knitters *par excellence* are Micky Shafer, Gina Kohler, Nancy Hewitt, Sally Thieszen, Karen Tadich, Jeanne Fangman, Joan Pickett, and Julie Richter. I could not do this without you, as you well know.

To all the yarn companies, I thank you for giving knitters everywhere magnificent yarns to choose from and for graciously providing some of them to bring my designs to life: Louet North America, Tahki Stacy Charles, South West Trading Company, Rowan/Westminster Fibers, Classic Elite Yarns, Plymouth Yarn Company, Cascade Yarns, Misti Alpaca, Blue Heron, and Skacel's Austermann, Schulana, and Zitron. I now have new yarn favorites to add to my longstanding ones.

As always, heartfelt gratitude goes to my family for their unbroken stream of encouragment and for letting me bury my head in the sand, er, yarn, while life goes on without me for a while. My husband Johnny, our son Alex, and daughter and son-in-law Justine and Jeffrey—thank you for being my rudder in the sea of book writing.

contents

THE LIGHT & LAYERED WOMAN

Today's woman is a modern maven of multi-tasking. As a whole, we have become experts at fluidly moving from one pursuit to the next with nary a moment to recalibrate our focus. We are passionate about all the things we do, bringing our giftedness into the mix of work and play. We want our wardrobes to speak of that mettle, and to reflect our personal styles.

My inspiration for this collection was to gather garments that every knitter wants to wear any day, anywhere, and in any season. With that goal in mind, I have designed a number of lightweight tops that are functional on so many levels that you'll return to them again and again to ante up to that perfect blend of feeling confident, comfortable, and chic. The garment designs are streamlined and figure flattering for enduring style, giving a healthy bolster to your valuable knitting time. Simple elegance defines each piece, whether it is designed for a close fit or loose drape.

> *Layering is the contemporary way to personalize style and expand function for comfort in any situation.*

Creative details promote a unique presentation—cables, raised stitches, pleats, and peplums define shape. Lace, intarsia, Fair Isle, and slip-stitch patterns offer challenges in knitting technique. The color palette is at times vivid and bold or neutral and subtle, and can always be personalized. I have used traditional knitting techniques in unusual ways and in combinations to give your wardrobe artistic panache.

These projects include yarns of linen, silk, bamboo, rayon, cotton, soy, and natural fibers of the non-wool variety, along with some beautiful synthetic novelty exceptions. They provide a solid foundation for building a wardrobe light enough to wear year round, next to the skin or in layers, for a variety of looks and styles.

Layering is the contemporary way to personalize style and expand function for comfort in any situation. Layers accommodate a variety of climates, seasonal temperature changes, daily fluctuations between the hot (or cold) outdoors and the cool (or warm) indoors, and even our own unreliable internal thermostats.

Layering also allows us to transiton between the activities of any given day—perhaps from business casual at work, followed by a sporting event, and then to a restaurant. Clearly, one style will not serve all events equally, but with thoughtfully selected key wardrobe pieces, you can easily change one or two outer pieces or accessories and completely change the look to fit the situation at hand.

The lightweight sweaters in this collection can go seamlessly from one look to another, simply by changing a wardrobe basic, such as from a pencil skirt to dress pants to a pair of jeans. The idea behind this, of course, is that the fabulous sweater you just knitted is the piece that is constant!

Knitting is certainly a lifestyle, and those of us who partake in it enjoy hours, which grow into years, of joyous activity. But wearing your knitting is a lifestyle all its own. There is a wealth of garment types, from classic traditionals to one-of-a-kind artful statements that may outfit only a single look. I believe that there is room for all of these pursuits. I will, however, entreat you to view a portion of your knitting as a wardrobe builder, so that you will have a selection of knitted basics to elevate the aesthetic of all potential ensemble coordinates.

IT BEGINS AND ENDS WITH FIT

We all tend to choose clothing that fits us best when deciding what to wear each day. And we all have examples of "almost-but-not-quite" garments that we never wear but refuse to get rid of. More often than not, a less-than-pleasing fit drives that garment back into the closet. Nothing ruins the success of a wardrobe faster than ill fit. With a multitude of accurate body measurements, knowledge of how to use your gauge, and a few tricks of the trade, you can achieve the right fit for you.

First, take accurate body measurements. At the very least, you need to know your bust/chest, waist, and hip circumferences, and the ideal lengths from hips to underarm and from underarm to shoulder. Also extremely helpful are the upper back width, arm length from the edge of the shoulder bone to the wrist bone when the arm is slightly bent, underarm to wrist bone with arm slightly bent, and underarm to the narrowest part of the waist. The more particular you are about the measurements, the better you can make adjustments to patterns for the best fit. One easy way to get the fit you like is to measure a favorite garment from your closet that fits perfectly. Take careful measurement and knit your own piece to the same dimensions.

Keep in mind that body measurements do not include ease—it's up to you to decide how much ease you want and to include it in the garment measurements. A close-fitting sweater is one that doesn't have much ease—it hugs the body and reveals all the curves. Such garments may actually measure one or two inches (2.5 to 5 cm) smaller than the body circumference so that they stretch for a body-conscious fit. If you'd rather have your garment hang a bit looser, add about 2" to 4" (5 to 10 cm) of ease to your body circumference. Add more ease if you'd like a very loose, baggy fit.

Second, you must know your gauge. Each pattern gives a gauge for the number of stitches in width and the number of rows in length of a 4" (10 cm) square. Knit a generous swatch and measure at least 4" (10 cm) in each direction to account for any partial stitches or rows per inch of fabric. If you use the yarn specified in the pattern and make sure your gauge matches that listed, your results with look like the photograph. But be aware that if you substitute a different yarn, you will alter the look, feel, and drape of the design. In these cases, you might want to make some changes.

If your gauge does not match that specified, you can adjust your needle size—larger needles create larger stitches and fewer stitches per inch; smaller needles create smaller stitches and more stitches per inch. If you change needle size and find that the resulting fabric is either too stiff or too loose, keep experimenting with needle size until you're happy with the hand and texture. Then, you can adjust the numbers in the pattern to fit your new gauge.

The numbers in the pattern that indicate stitch count may be adjusted for your new gauge through a simple formula, particularly if the design is straightforward without a lot of shaping. To adjust for a different gauge, divide your gauge (in stitches/inch) by the gauge specified in the pattern (also in stitches/inch) to find a conversion factor that you can use to adjust all the stitch numbers in the pattern.

For example, let's say that the pattern for a 36" (91.5 cm) pullover calls for 20 stitches/4" (10 cm) and you're getting a gauge of 22 stitches/4" (10 cm). Divide your gauge of 22 by the pattern gauge of 20 to get a conversion factor of 1.1%. If the pattern says to cast on 180 stitches, you'd multiply 180 by the conversion of 1.1% to determine the number of stitches you should cast on for your gauge:

180 stitches × 1.1% = 198 stitches

You would work the same conversion every time a number of stitches is specified in the pattern. However, keep in mind that this works best for simple shapes worked in simple stitch patterns. The formula won't work as well for designs that involve complicated silhouettes, textural stitch combinations, short-row shaping, or that require a specific number of rows. In these cases, unless you're prepared to do your own calculations, it's best to use the yarn indicated by the pattern and the size of needles that gives you the specified gauge.

Tips for Building Your Own Wardrobe

Although we all have closets full of garments, if you want to build a versatile wardrobe, all you need are ten pieces that you can mix, match, and layer, and you're set for two weeks of travel. Take a moment to be your own wardrobe consultant. To begin, draw a vertical line down a sheet of paper. On the left, list your main activities; on the right, list the types of clothing you'd like for each activity. Next, look for duplicates in the garment list, as well as pieces that would be worn with regularity. These are the garments to begin with—those that fit your personal lifestyle.

For example, a stay-at-home mom with small children may need mostly casual clothing that's comfortable but still gives a fashionable and chic appearance. Jeans, leggings, and cargo pants may all appeal, and if they are paired with a knitted shell or topped with a loose knitted tunic or cardigan, mom can go from play date to the grocery store to a casual restaurant to meet dad, all without changing a thing (unless sticky fingers are wiped on her pants along the way).

Knitting is definitely part of my lifestyle, but wearing that knitting takes something common and makes it uncommonly meaningful.

Consider a personal trainer and basketball coach, for a different example. This woman may spend most of her days in athletic clothes, but looks forward to switching from cross-trainers to chic pumps and throwing on a knitted tunic over her leggings to meet her beau for a movie date.

Are you an attorney who lives in a business suit? If that suit is cut for your proportions, it becomes sophisticated staging for a knitted silk shell. Through knitting, you can break the expected mold.

In our busy lives, our wardrobes should offer a backdrop for success, not a distraction to cramp our styles. Knitting is definitely part of my lifestyle, but wearing that knitting takes something common and makes it uncommonly meaningful.

renaissance

FINISHED SIZE
About 33 (36, 39, 42, 45, 48)" (84 [91.5, 99, 106.5, 114.5, 122] cm) bust circumference.
Pullover shown measures 36" (91.5 cm).

YARN
DK weight (#3 Light).
Shown here: Rowan Panama (55% rayon, 33% cotton, 12% linen; 148 yd [135 m]/50 g): #307 tulip (MC), 8 (8, 9, 10, 10, 11) balls; #306 begonia (A) and #305 dahlia (B), 1 ball each.

NEEDLES
Body and sleeves: size U.S. 4 (3.5 mm): 24" (60 cm) circular (cir).
Edging: size U.S. 3 (3.25 mm): 24" (60 cm) cir.
Adjust needle size if necessary to obtain the correct gauge.

NOTIONS
Markers (m); open-ring markers; waste yarn for holding sts; tapestry needle.

GAUGE
27 sts and 40 rows = 4" (10 cm) in St st on larger needle.

In the artistic rebirth of the fifteenth century, fabulously textured clothing is depicted in nearly every painting. This simple pullover pays homage to the heavier texture of the coarsely woven peasant shirts of the time. Knitted at a fine gauge with a blend of rayon, cotton, and linen, this version is shaped and lightweight and features a wide and somewhat square neckline that is the perfect foil for a bit of impromptu fancy: Fair Isle checks embellished with French knots and flanked by garter-stitch stripes. Jewelry is optional.

Change to larger needle and work even in St st (knit RS rows; purl WS rows) until piece measures 3" (7.5 cm) from CO, ending with a WS row.

Dec row: (RS) K1, k2tog, knit to last 3 sts, ssk, k1—2 sts dec'd.

Work 7 rows even.

Rep the last 8 rows 6 more times—105 (115, 125, 135, 145, 155) sts rem.

Cont even in St st until piece measures 11" (28 cm) from CO, ending with a WS row.

Inc row: (RS) K1, work left lifted inc (LLI; see Glossary) in next st, knit to last 2 sts, work right lifted inc (RLI; see Glossary) in next st, k1—2 sts inc'd.

Work 7 rows even.

Rep the last 8 rows once, then rep inc row once more—111 (121, 131, 141, 151, 161) sts. Work even until piece measures 15" (38 cm) from CO, ending with a WS row.

Shape Armholes

BO 5 sts at beg of next 0 (0, 0, 2, 2, 2) rows, then BO 4 sts at beg of foll 0 (2, 2, 2, 2, 4) rows, then BO 3 sts at beg of foll 2 (2, 2, 0, 0, 0) rows, then BO 2 sts at beg of foll 6 (6, 6, 8, 8, 8) rows, then BO 1 st at beg of foll 2 rows—91 (93, 103, 105, 115, 117) sts rem.

Place sts onto waste-yarn holder.

FRONT

CO and work as for back.

RIGHT SLEEVE

With MC and smaller needle, CO 75 (75, 81, 89, 91, 91 sts. Do not join.

Set-up row: (WS) [P1, k1] 18 (18, 20, 23, 24, 24) times, p1, place marker (pm), p15, pm, [p1, k1] 11 (11, 12, 13, 13, 13) times, p1.

Row 1: (RS) [K1, p1] 11 (11, 12, 13, 13, 13) times, k1, slip marker (sl m), k15, sl m, [k1, p1] 18 (18, 20, 23, 24, 23) times, k1.

BACK

With MC and smaller needle, CO 119 (129, 139, 149, 159, 169) sts. Do not join for working in rnds.

Set-up row: (WS) *P1, k1; rep from * to last st, p1.

Next row: (RS) *K1, p1; rep from * to last st, k1.

Rep set-up row once more.

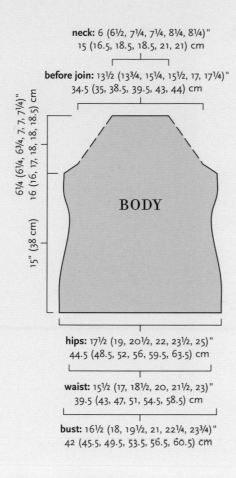

neck: 6 (6½, 7¼, 7¼, 8¼, 8¼)"
15 (16.5, 18.5, 18.5, 21, 21) cm

before join: 13½ (13¾, 15¼, 15½, 17, 17¼)"
34.5 (35, 38.5, 39.5, 43, 44) cm

6¼ (6¼, 6¾, 7, 7, 7¼)"
16 (16, 17, 18, 18, 18.5) cm

15" (38 cm)

BODY

hips: 17½ (19, 20½, 22, 23½, 25)"
44.5 (48.5, 52, 56, 59.5, 63.5) cm

waist: 15½ (17, 18½, 20, 21½, 23)"
39.5 (43, 47, 51, 54.5, 58.5) cm

bust: 16½ (18, 19½, 21, 22¼, 23¾)"
42 (45.5, 49.5, 53.5, 56.5, 60.5) cm

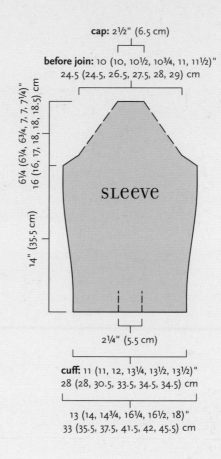

cap: 2½" (6.5 cm)

before join: 10 (10, 10½, 10¾, 11, 11½)"
24.5 (24.5, 26.5, 27.5, 28, 29) cm

6¼ (6¼, 6¾, 7, 7, 7¼)"
16 (16, 17, 18, 18, 18.5) cm

14" (35.5 cm)

SLEEVE

2¼" (5.5 cm)

cuff: 11 (11, 12, 13¼, 13½, 13½)"
28 (28, 30.5, 33.5, 34.5, 34.5) cm

13 (14, 14¾, 16¼, 16½, 18)"
33 (35.5, 37.5, 41.5, 42, 45.5) cm

Row 2: (WS): [P1, k1] 18 (18, 20, 23, 24, 24) times, p1, sl m, p15, sl m, [p1, k1] 11 (11, 12, 13, 13, 13) times, p1.

Change to larger needle and work even in St st until piece measures 2" (5 cm) from CO, ending with a WS row.

Replace markers with open-ring markers between stitches in fabric to define pleat placement.

Inc row: (RS) K1, work LLI in next st, knit to last 2 sts, work RLI in next st, k1—2 sts inc'd.

Work 15 (11, 11, 11, 11, 7) rows even.

Rep the last 16 (12, 12, 12, 12, 8) rows 5 (9, 8, 9, 9, 14) more times—87 (95, 99, 109, 111, 121) sts.

Work even until piece measures 14" (35.5 cm) from CO, ending with a WS row.

Shape Cap

BO 5 sts at beg of next 0 (0, 0, 2, 2, 2) rows, then BO 4 sts at beg of foll 0 (2, 2, 2, 2, 4) rows, then BO 3 sts at beg of foll 2 (2, 2, 0, 0, 0) rows, then BO 2 sts at beg of foll 6 (6, 6, 8, 8, 8) rows, then BO 1 st at beg of foll 2 rows—67 (67, 71, 73, 75, 77) sts rem.

Place sts onto waste-yarn holder.

LEFT SLEEVE

With MC and smaller needle, CO 75 (75, 81, 89, 91, 91) sts. Do not join.

Set-up row: (WS) [P1, k1] 11 (11, 12, 13, 13, 13) times, p1, pm, p15, pm, [p1, k1] 18 (18, 20, 23, 24, 24) times, p1.

Row 1: (RS) [K1, p1] 18 (18, 20, 22, 23, 23) times, k1, sl m, k15, sl m, [k1, p1] 11 (11, 12, 13, 13, 13) times, k1.

Row 2: (WS) [P1, k1] 11 (11, 12, 13, 13, 13) times, p1, sl m, p15, sl m, [p1, k1] 18 (18, 20, 23, 24, 24) times, p1.

Change to larger needle and work even in St st until piece measures 2" (5 cm) from CO, ending with a WS row.

Replace markers with open-ring markers between stitches in fabric to define pleat placement.

Inc row: (RS) K1, work LLI in next st, knit to last 2 sts, work RLI in next st, k1—2 sts inc'd.

Work 15 (11, 11, 11, 11, 7) rows even.

Rep the last 16 (12, 12, 12, 12, 8) rows 5 (9, 8, 9, 9, 14) more times—87 (95, 99, 109, 111, 121) sts.

Work even until piece measures 14" (35.5 cm) from CO, ending with a WS row.

Shape Cap

BO 5 sts at beg of next 0 (0, 0, 2, 2, 2) rows, then BO 4 sts at beg of foll 0 (2, 2, 2, 2, 4) rows, then BO 3 sts at beg of foll 2 (2, 2, 0, 0, 0) rows, then BO 2 sts at beg of foll 6 (6, 6, 8, 8, 8) rows, then BO 1 st at beg of foll 2 rows—67 (67, 71, 73, 75, 77) sts rem.

Place sts on waste yarn holder.

YOKE

With RS facing, place all pieces on larger needle as foll: 91 (93, 103, 105, 115, 117) back sts, 67 (67, 71, 73, 75, 77), left sleeve sts, pm, 91 (93, 103, 105, 115, 117) front sts, pm, 67 (67, 71, 73, 75, 77) right sleeve sts—316 (320, 348, 356, 380, 388) sts total.

Pm and join for working in rnds.

Dec rnd: *K1, ssk, knit to 3 sts before next m, k2tog, k1, sl m; rep from * 3 more times—8 sts dec'd.

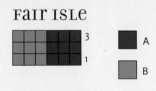

FAIR ISLE

■ A

■ B

Next rnd: Knit.

Rep the last 2 rnds 18 (18, 20, 21, 22, 23) more times—164 (168, 180, 180, 196, 196) sts rem; 53 (55, 61, 61, 69, 69) sts each for back and front, 29 sts for each sleeve.

Change to A and work as foll:

Rnd 1: *K1, ssk, knit to 3 sts before next m, k2tog, k1, sl m; rep from * 3 more times—8 sts dec'd.

Rnd 2: Purl.

Change to B and rep the last 2 rnds.

Change to MC and rep Rnd 1.

Next rnd: Purl and *at the same time* dec 1 (0, 0, 0, 2, 2) sts evenly spaced in the back and again in the front—138 (144, 156, 156, 168, 168) sts rem; 46 (49, 55, 55, 61, 61) sts each in front and back, 23 sts in each sleeve.

Work Rnds 1–3 of Fair Isle chart.

Next rnd: With MC, *k1, ssk, knit to 3 sts before next m, k2tog, k1, sl m; rep from * 3 more times—8 sts dec'd.

Next rnd: Purl.

Change to B and rep the last 2 rnds once.

Next rnd: With A, *k1, ssk, knit to 3 sts before next m, k2tog, k1, sl m; rep from * 3 more times—114 (120, 132, 132, 144, 144) sts rem.

BO all sts purlwise.

FINISHING

With WS facing, steam-block (see Glossary) garment. Lay flat and allow to air-dry thoroughly before moving.

Cuff Pleats

Fold lower edge of sleeve with RS facing tog, matching edges of St st at center of ribbing between open-ring markers. With about 12" (30.5 cm) of MC threaded on a tapestry needle, RS facing, and using the mattress st for St st (see Glossary) leaving a 6" (15 cm) tail, sew pleat for 1¾" (4.5 cm) up from CO edge. Insert needle to WS and use a single whipstitch (see Glossary) to secure in place. Thread 6" (15 cm) tail onto a tapestry needle and whipstitch all layers tog along CO edge, placing pleat fold toward front of sleeve.

Steam-block pleat to set seams.

Seams

With yarn threaded on a tapestry needle, use the mattress st with ½-st seam allowance (see Glossary) to sew side and sleeve seams. Steam seams from WS.

Turn sleeves RS out and, with RS facing tog and matching armhole shaping, pin sleeves into armholes.

Know Your Yarn: Cotton

Cotton is a soft fluffy fiber that grows in a boll, a protective capsule on a cotton shrub. It is almost pure cellulose. Cotton has been cultivated since antiquity, with some of the earliest fabric evidence seen in Pakistan from at least 5,000 B.C.

American Eli Whitney's invention of the cotton gin lowered the cost of production and led to widespread use of cotton for textiles and other goods. Cotton is now the most used fiber for textiles worldwide.

Cotton fibers have good dimensional stability and are uniform in size and shape. Cotton fabrics and yarn are sturdy, durable, and long lasting. Cotton takes dye well and has good color retention, and is easily laundered by machine. As a yarn, it is easy to handle; as a garment it is soft, breathable, and extremely comfortable.

Use slip-st crochet (see Glossary) to join the pieces tog. Steam seams from WS.

Embroidery

With MC threaded on a tapestry needle, work a French knot (see Glossary) centered in each Fair Isle square around the neckline, bringing needle up from WS to the right of the center st in Row 3 of the charted patt, work a French knot, then insert needle to WS to the left of the center st in the same row.

Weave in loose ends. Steam from WS to set sts.

PIER 39

FINISHED SIZE
About 34 (36, 38, 40)" (86.5 [91.5, 96.5, 101.5] cm) bust circumference.
Shell shown measures 34" (86.5 cm).

YARN
DK weight (#3 Light).
Shown here: Filatura di Crosa Brilla (42% cotton, 58% viscose rayon; 120 yd [110 m]/50 g): #391 red, 8 (9, 10, 11) balls.

NEEDLES
Body: size U.S. 6 (4.5 mm): 24" (60 cm) circular (cir).
Edging: size U.S. 4 (3.5 mm): 24" (60 cm) cir and extra needle the same size or smaller for three-needle bind-off.
Adjust needle size if necessary to obtain the correct gauge.

NOTIONS
Markers (m); stitch holders; size E/4 (3.5 mm) crochet hook; tapestry needle.

GAUGE
24 sts and 27 rows = 4" (10 cm) in St st on larger needle.

A solid-color shaped shell is an indispensible wardrobe basic. This streamlined design with puzzle-piece construction makes for an adventure in knitting that is not for the faint-hearted. Shaped pieces and cable borders with short-row shaping are knitted separately and sewn together. While the keyhole in the back reflects classic style, the elongated front keyhole is unexpectedly bold for what is generally considered to be an understated garment. Worn layered under a shaped, structured suit jacket, it is a bold pop of color with visual texture that tosses "plain" out the window.

BACK

With smaller needle, CO 119 (125, 131, 137) sts. Do not join for working in rnds.

Set-up row: (WS) P1, k1, *p1 through back loop (tbl), k1; rep from * to last st, p1.

Row 1: (RS) K1, p1, *k1tbl, p1; rep from * to last st, k1.

Row 2: P1, k1, *p1tbl, k1; rep from * to last st, p1.

Rep the last 2 rows once, then work Row 1 once more.

Next row: (WS) Purl and *at the same time* dec 12 sts evenly spaced—107 (113, 119, 125) sts rem.

Change to larger needle work 8 rows even in St st.

Dec row: (RS) K1, k2tog, knit to last 3 sts, ssk, k1—2 sts dec'd.

Work 5 rows even.

Rep the last 6 rows 4 more times, then rep dec row once more—95 (101, 107, 113) sts rem.

Work 15 (17, 19, 21) rows even.

Inc row: (RS) K1, work left lifted inc (LLI; see Glossary) in next st, knit to last 2 sts, work right lifted inc (RLI; see Glossary) in next st, k1—2 sts inc'd.

Work 7 rows even. Rep the last 8 rows once, then rep inc row once more—101 (107, 113, 119) sts.

Work even until piece measures 13½ (13¾, 14, 14¼)" (34.5 [35, 35.5, 36] cm) from CO, ending with a WS row.

Shape Right Armhole and Keyhole

NOTE: Keyhole shaping is introduced while armhole shaping is in progress; read all the way through the following sections before proceeding.

At right armhole edge (beg of RS rows), BO 5 sts 0 (0, 0, 1) time, then BO 4 sts once, then BO 3 sts 0 (1, 2, 2) time(s), then BO 2 sts 1 (1, 1, 0) time—6 (9, 12, 15) armhole sts BO.

Dec row: (RS) K1, k2tog, knit to end—1 st dec'd.

Purl 1 WS row. Rep the last 2 rows once.

Rep dec row, then work 11 rows even. Rep the last 12 rows once, then rep dec once more—5 more armhole sts dec'd total.

At the same time shape keyhole as foll:

Use an open-ring marker to mark center st.

Beg on same row as first armhole BO, knit to center, including marked center st. Place rem sts on holder to work later for left armhole.

Next row: BO 1 st pwise for keyhole, purl to end—back is split into two sides.

Cont shaping right armhole and work keyhole as foll:

Dec Row 1: (RS) Working armhole shaping as established, knit to last 3 sts, k2tog, k1—1 keyhole st dec'd.

Dec Row 2: (WS) P1, p2tog, purl to end—1 keyhole st dec'd.

Rep the last 2 rows 4 more times—10 sts dec'd at keyhole in 10 rows.

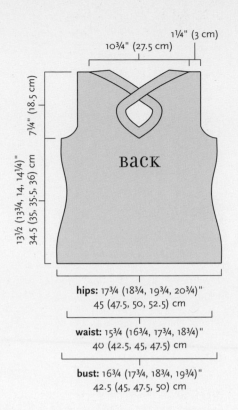

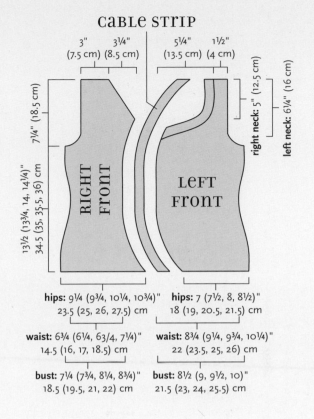

CABLE STRIP

Back diagram labels:
1¼" (3 cm)
10¾" (27.5 cm)
7¼" (18.5 cm)
13½ (13¾, 14, 14¼)" 34.5 (35, 35.5, 36) cm

BACK

hips: 17¾ (18¾, 19¾, 20¾)"
45 (47.5, 50, 52.5) cm

waist: 15¾ (16¾, 17¾, 18¾)"
40 (42.5, 45, 47.5) cm

bust: 16¾ (17¾, 18¾, 19¾)"
42.5 (45, 47.5, 50) cm

Right/Left front diagram labels:
3" (7.5 cm) 3¼" (8.5 cm) 5¼" (13.5 cm) 1½" (4 cm)
right neck: 5" (12.5 cm)
left neck: 6¼" (16 cm)
7¼" (18.5 cm)
13½ (13¾, 14, 14¼)" 34.5 (35, 35.5, 36) cm

RIGHT FRONT

LEFT FRONT

hips: 9¼ (9¾, 10¼, 10¾)"
23.5 (25, 26, 27.5) cm

waist: 6¾ (6¼, 6¾, 7¼)"
14.5 (16, 17, 18.5) cm

bust: 7¼ (7¾, 8¼, 8¾)"
18.5 (19.5, 21, 22) cm

hips: 7 (7½, 8, 8½)"
18 (19, 20.5, 21.5) cm

waist: 8¾ (9¼, 9¾, 10¼)"
22 (23.5, 25, 26) cm

bust: 8½ (9, 9½, 10)"
21.5 (23, 24, 25.5) cm

Rep Dec Row 1 once again, then purl 1 row even. Rep the last 2 rows 3 more times—4 more keyhole sts dec'd.

Work 4 (4, 6, 8) rows even.

Inc Row 1: (RS) Knit to last 2 sts, work LLI in next st, k1—1 keyhole st inc'd.

Inc Row 2: (WS) P1, work LLI purlwise in next st, purl to end—1 keyhole st inc'd.

Rep the last 2 rows once, then rep Inc Row 1 once again—5 keyhole sts total inc'd.

Next row: (WS) Use the backward-loop method (see Glossary) to CO 2 sts, purl these 2 sts tbl, then purl to end—2 keyhole sts inc'd.

Knit 1 RS row.

Rep the last 2 rows once more—4 keyhole sts total CO.

Shape Right Neck

At neck edge (beg of WS rows) and working purlwise, BO 2 sts 2 times, then BO 3 sts 5 times, then BO 4 sts 2 times—7 sts rem for all sizes.

Place sts on holder.

Shape Left Armhole and Keyhole

NOTE: Keyhole shaping is introduced while armhole shaping is in progress; read all the way through the following sections before proceeding.

Transfer held back sts to larger cir needle. Join yarn at center edge.

At left armhole edge, (beg of WS rows), BO 5 sts 0 (0, 0, 1) time, then BO 4 sts once, then BO 3 sts 0 (1, 2, 2) time(s), then BO 2 sts 1 (1, 1, 0) time—6 (9, 12, 15) armhole sts BO.

Dec row: (RS) Knit to last 3 sts, ssk, k1—1 st dec'd.

Purl 1 WS row. Rep the last 2 rows once.

Rep dec row, then work 11 rows even. Rep the last 12 rows once, then rep dec row once more—5 armhole sts total dec'd.

At the same time beg on RS row foll first armhole BO, shape keyhole as foll:

Dec Row 1: (RS) K1, ssk, knit to end—1 keyhole st dec'd.

Dec Row 2: (WS) Working armhole shaping as established, purl to last 3 sts, ssp (see Glossary), p1—1 keyhole st dec'd.

Rep the last 2 rows 4 more times—10 sts dec'd at keyhole in 10 rows.

Rep Dec Row 1 once again, then purl 1 row even. Rep the last 2 rows 3 more times—4 more keyhole sts dec'd.

Work 4 (4, 6, 8) rows even.

Inc Row 1: (RS) K1, work RLI in next st, knit to end—1 keyhole st inc'd.

Inc Row 2: (WS) Purl to last 2 sts, RLI purlwise in next st, p1—1 keyhole st inc'd.

Rep the last 2 rows once, then rep Inc Row 1 once again—5 keyhole sts total inc'd.

Purl 1 row even.

Next row: (RS) Use the backward-loop method to CO 2 sts, knit to end—2 keyhole sts inc'd.

Purl 1 WS row. Rep the last 2 rows once more—4 keyhole sts total CO.

Shape Left Neck

At neck edge (beg of RS rows) BO 2 sts 2 times, then BO 3 sts 5 times, then BO 4 sts 2 times—7 sts rem for all sizes.

Place sts on holder.

RIGHT FRONT

With smaller cir needle CO 67 (71, 73, 77) sts.

Set-up row: (WS) P1, k1, *p1tbl, k1; rep from * to last st, p1.

Row 1: (RS) K1, k2tog, p1, *k1tbl, p1; rep from * to last st, k1—1 st dec'd.

Row 2: P1, k1, *p1tbl, k1; rep from * to last 3 sts, ssk, p1—1 st dec'd.

Row 3: K1, k2tog, p1, *k1tbl, p1; rep from * to last st, k1—1 st dec'd.

Row 4: P1, k1, *p1tbl, k1; rep from * to last 3 sts, ssk, p1—1 st dec'd.

Row 5: K1, k2tog, p1, *k1tbl, p1; rep from * to last st, k1—62 (66, 68, 72) sts rem.

Row 6: Purl and *at the same time* dec 6 (7, 6, 7) sts evenly spaced—56 (59, 62, 65) sts rem.

Change to larger needle and St st.

Shape Center Front

NOTE: Side, center front, armhole, and neck shaping are worked simultaneously; read all the way through the following sections before proceeding.

Dec row: (RS) K1, k2tog, knit to end—1 st dec'd.

Dec 1 st at center front in this manner every RS row 8 more times.

[Rep dec row, then work 3 rows even] 4 times.

Rep dec row, work 5 rows even, then rep dec row—15 center front sts total dec'd.

Work 15 (17, 19, 21) rows even.

Inc row: (RS) K1, work RLI in next st, work to end—1 st inc'd.

Work 9 rows even.

Rep inc row, then work 5 rows even. Rep the last 6 rows 4 more times.

RS Inc Row: (RS) Rep inc row—1 st inc'd.

WS Inc Row: (WS) Purl to last 2 sts, work RLI purlwise in next st, p1—1 st inc'd.

Rep the last 2 rows once, then rep WS inc row once more—11 center front sts total inc'd.

Shape Neck

Dec row: (RS) Sl 1 kwise, k2tog, knit to end—1 st dec'd.

Purl 1 row.

Rep the last 2 rows 19 more times—20 neck sts total dec'd.

Work even until armhole measures same as back.

BO all sts.

Shape Side

At the same time working center front, neck, and armhole shaping as specified, shape the side as foll:

Work 8 rows in St st above lower rib.

Dec row: (RS) Work to last 3 sts, ssk, k1—1 st dec'd.

Work 5 rows even. Rep the last 6 rows 4 more times, then work dec row once again—6 side sts total dec'd.

Work 15 (17, 19, 21) rows even.

Inc row: (RS) Work to last 3 sts, work RLI in next st, k1—1 st inc'd.

Work 7 rows even. Rep the last 8 rows once, then rep inc row once more—3 more side sts inc'd.

Work even until piece measures 13½ (13¾, 14, 14¼)" (34.5 [35, 35.5, 36] cm), ending with a WS row.

Shape Armhole

At armhole edge (beg of WS rows), BO 5 sts 0 (0, 0, 1) time, then BO 4 sts once, then BO 3 sts 0 (1, 2, 2) time(s), then BO 2 sts 1 (1, 1, 0) time—6 (9, 12, 15) armhole sts BO.

Dec row: (RS) Work to last 3 sts, ssk, k1—1 st dec'd.

Purl 1 WS row. Rep the last 2 rows once more.

[Rep dec row, work 11 rows even] 2 times, then rep dec row once again—5 more armhole sts dec'd.

Work armhole edge even until neck shaping is complete—18 sts rem after all center front, side, armhole, and neck shaping is complete.

LEFT FRONT

With smaller cir needle CO 41 (45, 47, 51) sts.

Set-up row: (WS) P1, k1, *p1tbl, k1; rep from * to last st, p1.

Row 1: (RS) K1, *p1, k1tbl; rep from * to last 2 sts, p1, M1 (see Glossary), k1—1 st inc'd.

Row 2: P1, M1, p1, *k1, p1tbl; rep from * to last 2 sts, k1, p1—1 st inc'd.

Row 3: K1, *p1, k1tbl; rep from * to last 2 sts, p1, M1, k1—1 st inc'd.

Row 4: P1, M1, p1, *k1, p1tbl; rep from * to last 2 sts, k1, p1—1 st inc'd.

Row 5: K1, *p1, k1tbl; rep from * to last 2 sts, p1, M1, k1—46 (50, 52, 56) sts.

Row 6: Purl and *at the same time* dec 4 (5, 4, 5) sts evenly spaced—42 (45, 48, 51) sts rem.

Shape Center Front

....
NOTE: Side, center front, armhole, and neck shaping are worked simultaneously; read all the way through the following sections before proceeding.
....

Change to larger needle and St st.

Inc row: (RS) Work to last st, M1, k1—1 st inc'd.

Inc 1 st in this manner every RS row 8 more times.

Dec row: (RS) K1, k2tog, knit to end—1 st dec'd.

Work 5 rows even. Rep the last 6 rows 4 more times, then work dec row once more—6 side sts dec'd total.

Work 15 (17, 19, 21) rows even.

Inc row: (RS) Work to last 3 sts, LLI in next st, k1—1 st inc'd.

Work 7 rows even. Rep the last 8 rows once, then rep inc row once more—3 more side sts inc'd.

Work even until piece measures 13½ (13¾, 14, 14¼)" (34.5 [35, 35.5, 36] cm), ending with a WS row.

Shape Armhole

At armhole edge (beg of RS rows), BO 5 sts 0 (0, 0, 1) time, then BO 4 sts once, then BO 3 sts 0 (1, 2, 2) time(s), then BO 2 sts 1 (1, 1, 0) time—6 (9, 12, 15) armhole sts BO.

Dec row: (RS) K1, k2tog, knit to end—1 st dec'd.

Purl 1 WS row. Rep the last 2 rows once more.

[Rep dec row, work 11 rows even] 2 times, then rep dec row once again—5 more armhole sts dec'd.

Work armhole edge even until neck shaping is complete—9 sts rem.

BO all sts.

FRONT CABLE STRIP

With smaller needle, CO 10 sts.

Set-up row: (WS) P1, k1, p6, k1, p1.

Cont in short-rows (see Glossary) as foll:

Short-Row 1: With RS facing, k1, p1, k2, wrap next st, turn work so WS is facing, p2, k1, p1.

Short-Row 2: With RS facing and working wrap tog with wrapped st when you come to it, k1, p1, k4, wrap next st, turn work so WS is facing, p4, k1, p1.

Short-Row 3: With RS facing and working wrap tog with wrapped st when you come to it, k1, p1, k6, wrap next st, turn work so WS is facing, p6, k1, p1.

Next row: (RS cable row) K1, p1, sl 3 sts onto cn and hold in back of work, k3, then k3 from cn, p1, k1.

[Rep inc row, then work 3 rows even] 4 times.

[Rep inc row, then work 5 rows even] 3 times.

Rep inc row, then work 11 (13, 15, 17) rows even—17 center front sts total inc'd.

Dec row: (RS) Work to last 3 sts, ssk, k1—1 st dec'd.

Work 5 rows even. Rep the last 6 rows 4 more times—5 center front sts total dec'd.

Work 1 RS row.

Shape Neck

At neck edge (beg of WS rows) and working purlwise, BO 4 sts 3 times, then BO 3 sts once, then BO 2 sts 3 times—21 neck sts BO.

Dec row: (WS) Sl 1, p1, psso, purl to end—1 st dec'd.

Work 1 row even. Rep the last 2 rows 5 more times, then [rep dec row, then work 3 rows even] 4 times—10 more neck sts dec'd.

Shape Side

At the same time working center front, neck, and armhole shaping as specified, shape the side as foll:

Work 8 rows in St st above lower rib.

Work 5 rows even in patt as established.

Maintaining 6-row cable patt, rep the last 6 rows until piece measures 15½ (15¾, 16, 16¼)" (39.5 [40, 40.5, 41.5] cm) from CO, measured along right edge of strip.

Next row: (RS) Sl 1 purlwise with yarn in back (pwise wyb), p1, work 6 sts as established, p1, k1.

Cont in patt as established until piece measures 16½ (16¾, 17, 17¼)" (42 [42.5, 43, 44] cm) from CO, measured along left edge of strip, ending with a RS row.

Next row: (WS) Sl 1 pwise with yarn in front (wyf,) k1, p6, k1, p1.

NOTE: Following the slipped st on the right-hand edge of the cable band, when transferring yarn to opposite side in preparation for the second st, pull snugly to maintain slipped-st integrity along the edge.

Slipping the first st of every row, cont in patt as established until piece measures about 22½ (22¾, 23, 23¼)"(54.5 [58, 58.5, 59] cm) from CO, measured along left edge of strip when slightly stretched.

BO all sts in patt.

LEFT FRONT NECK EDGE CABLE STRIP

With smaller needle, CO 10 sts.

Set-up row: (WS) P1, k1, p6, k1, p1.

Row 1: (RS) K1, p1, k6, p1, k1.

Row 2: Sl 1 pwise wyf , k1, p6, k1, p1.

Row 3: (cable row) K1, p1, sl 3 sts onto cn and hold in back of work, k3, then k3 from cn, p1, k1.

Rows 4, 5, 6, 7, and 8: Work even in patt as established.

Rep Rows 3–8 until piece measures about 10 (10, 10¼, 10½)" (25.5 [25.5, 26, 26.5] cm) from CO, or long enough to fit around left front neck edge when slightly stretched.

BO all sts.

RIGHT BACK KEYHOLE CABLE STRIP

NOTE: This strip will attach to the left shoulder.

With smaller needle, CO 10 sts.

Set-up row: (WS) P1, k1, p6, k1, p1.

Row 1: (RS) K1, p1, k6, p1, k1.

Row 2: Sl 1 pwise wyf, k1, p6, k1, p1.

Row 3: (cable row) K1, p1, sl 3 sts onto cn and hold to front of work, k3, then k3 from cn, p1, k1.

Rows 4, 5, 6, 7, and 8: Work even in patt as established.

Rep Rows 3–8 two more times.

***Next row:** Rep Row 3.

Next row: P1, k1, p6, k1, p1.

Work short-rows as foll:

Short-Row 1: (counts as Rows 5 and 6 of cable patt) With RS facing, k1, p1, k6, wrap next st, turn work so WS is facing, p6, k1, p1.

Short-Row 2: (counts as Rows 7 and 8 of cable patt) With RS facing, k1, p1, k3, wrap next st, turn work so WS is facing, p3, k1, p1.

Rep from * 3 more times.

[Rep Row 3, then work 5 rows even] 3 times.

Rep Row 3, then work 1 WS row.

Next row: (RS) Sl 1 pwise wyb, p1, work 6 sts as established, p1, k1.

Discontinue slipping first st on WS rows (purl first st instead to end of cable strip) and cont in patt until piece measures about 11½ (11½, 11¾, 12)" (29 [29, 30, 30.5] cm) from CO, or long enough to fit around right edge of keyhole and left back neck when slightly stretched, measured along right-hand edge and ending with a WS row.

At beg of RS rows, BO 3 sts 2 times, then BO rem 4 sts.

LEFT BACK KEYHOLE CABLE STRIP

NOTE: This strip will attach to the right shoulder.

With smaller needle, CO 10 sts.

Set-up row: (WS) P1, k1, p6, k1, p1.

Row 1: (RS) Sl 1 kwise, p1, k6, p1, k1.

Row 2: P1, k1, p6, k1, p1.

Row 3: (cable row) Sl 1 kwise, p1, sl 3 sts onto cn and hold in back of work, k3, then k3 from cn, p1, k1.

Rows 4, 5, 6, 7, and 8: Work even in patt as established.

Rep Rows 3–8 two more times.

*Next row:** Rep Row 3.

Work short-rows as foll:

Short-Row 1: (counts as Rows 4 and 5 of cable patt) With WS facing, p1, k1, p6, wrap next st, turn work so RS is facing, k6, p1, k1.

Short-Row 2: (counts as Rows 6 and 7 of cable patt) With WS facing, p1, k1, p3, wrap next st, turn work so RS is facing, k3, p1, k1.

Next row: P1, k1, p6, k1, p1.

Rep from * 3 more times.

[Rep Row 3, then work 5 rows even] 3 times, then rep Row 3 again.

Next row: (WS) Sl 1 pwise wyf, k1, p6, k1, p1.

Discontinue slipping first st on RS rows (knit this st instead to end of cable strip), cont in patt as established until piece measures about 11½ (11½, 11 ¾, 12)" (29 [29, 30, 30.5] cm) from CO, or long enough to fit around left edge of keyhole and right back neck when slightly stretched, measured along left-hand edge and ending with a RS row.

At beg of WS rows, BO 3 sts 2 times, then BO rem 4 sts.

FINISHING

Using the wet-towel method (see Glossary), block pieces to measurements. Allow to air-dry thoroughly before moving.

Attach Cable Strips

NOTE: See illustrations for assembly directions.

With yarn threaded on a tapestry needle and using a mattress st (see Glossary), sew left back keyhole cable to left back, aligning left edge of strip to right edge of keyhole, and right edge of strip to V-neck edge of right back so that end of strip is even with right back shoulder (**Figure 1**).

Sew right back keyhole cable to right back, aligning right edge of strip to left edge of keyhole, overlapping left back keyhole cable, and aligning left edge of strip to V-neck edge of left back, so that end of strip is even with left back shoulder (**Figure 2**).

Sew center front cable strip to right front curved edge, beg at hem and ending at base of V-neck (**Figure 3**).

Sew left front cable strip to left front, beg at center neck edge and ending at shoulder (**Figure 4**).

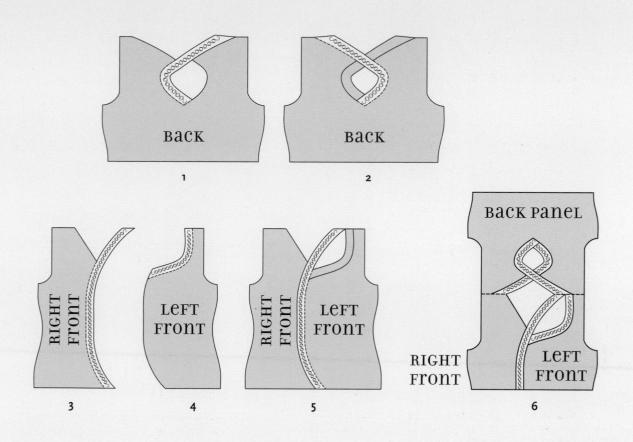

Sew center front strip to center left front edge, beg at hem and ending at top edge of left front cable strip **(Figure 5)**.

Seams

With RS facing tog and working from the WS, use slip-st crochet (see Glossary) to join front to back at shoulders, catching the end of the center front cable strip along the left shoulder seam **(Figure 6)**.

With yarn threaded on a tapestry needle and using the mattress st, sew side seams.

Steam seams to set sts.

Armbands

With smaller cir needle, RS facing, and beg at base of armhole, pick up and knit 78 (86, 92, 100) sts evenly spaced around armhole. BO all sts pwise.

Weave in loose ends. Steam armbands to set sts.

TAILOReD PLeaTS

FINISHED SIZE
About 32 (34, 36, 38, 40, 42, 44, 46)" (81.5 [86.5 ,91.5, 96.5, 101.5, 106.5, 112, 117] cm) bust circumference.
Pullover shown measures 36" (91.5 cm).

YARN
DK weight (#3 Light).
Shown here: Skacel Schulana Seda-Mar (88% silk, 12% nylon; 180 yd [165 m]/50 g): #26 gold (MC), 7 (7, 7, 7, 7, 8, 8, 9) balls; #12 dark rust (CC), 1 ball.

NEEDLES
Size U.S. 6 (4 mm): 24" (60 cm) circular (cir).
Adjust needle size if necessary to obtain the correct gauge.

NOTIONS
Stitch holders; markers (m); cable needle (cn); size G/4 (4 mm) crochet hook; tapestry needle.

GAUGE
22 sts and 28 rows = 4" (10 cm) in St st.

The classic V-neck pullover gets a contemporary tweak in this sophisticated top. Featuring a shaped waist amplified with triangular inverted pleats, this streamlined design has a graceful flare around the hemline and cuffs. A rolled stockinette-stitch collar frames the V-neck, and a bit of rib at the back neck encourages it to stand up. Worked in an exquisite silk tape yarn, this top is the ultimate in smooth texture and soft drape. An accent of color at the hem and cuffs provides stylish but understated contrast. Wear it alone or under a suit jacket for the office, or with a beaded Chanel for the opera.

BACK

NOTE: Side shaping is introduced at the same time as gore pleats are worked; read all the way through the following section before proceeding.

With CC, CO 139 (145, 145, 151, 151, 157, 157, 163) sts. Do not join for working in rnds.

Change to MC and knit 1 RS row.

Set-up row: (WS) *[P1, k1] 16 (17, 17, 18, 18, 19, 19, 20) times, p1, place marker (pm), k20, pm; rep from * once, [p1, k1] 16 (17, 17, 18, 18, 19, 19, 20) times, p1.

Row 1: (RS) *K33 (35, 35, 37, 37, 39, 39, 41), slip marker (sl m), p20, sl m; rep from * once, knit to end.

Row 2: *P33 (35, 35, 37, 37, 39, 39, 41), sl m, k20, sl m; rep from * once, purl to end.

Rep the last 2 rows once more.

Shape Gore Pleats

Dec row: (RS) *K33 (35, 35, 37, 37, 39, 39, 41), sl m, p2tog, purl to 2 sts before next m, ssp (see Glossary), sl m; rep from * once, knit to end—4 sts dec'd.

Work 3 rows even in patt as established. Rep the last 4 rows 8 more times—2 purl sts will rem at top of gore pleat.

Work 4 rows even as established.

Next row: (RS) Knit to 1 st before m, *ssk (remove m to work the dec, then replace m before the dec on the right needle), k2tog (remove m to work the dec, then replace m after the dec on right needle)—2 sts between markers*, knit to 1 st before m; rep from * to * once, knit to end—4 sts dec'd.

Work 1 WS row even.

Next row: (RS) *Knit to m, remove m, work button st (see Stitch Guide) over next 2 sts; rep from * once, knit to end.

At the same time after working 6 rows past the set-up row, shape sides as foll:

***Dec row:** K1, ssk, work as established to last 3 sts, k2tog, k1—2 side sts dec'd.

Work 5 rows even, rep dec row, then work 3 rows even; rep from * 3 (3, 3, 3, 1, 2, 0, 0) more time(s)—16 (16, 16, 16, 8, 12, 4, 4) sts dec'd at side edges.

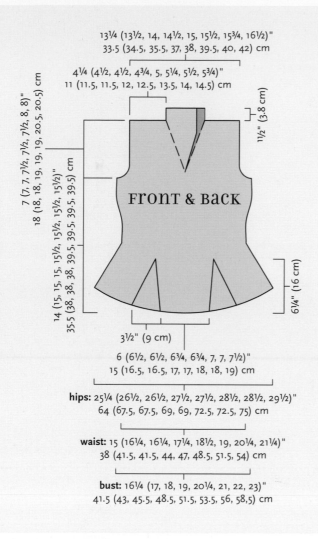

13¼ (13½, 14, 14½, 15, 15½, 15¾, 16½)"
33.5 (34.5, 35.5, 37, 38, 39.5, 40, 42) cm
4¼ (4½, 4½, 4¾, 5, 5¼, 5½, 5¾)"
11 (11.5, 11.5, 12, 12.5, 13.5, 14, 14.5) cm
1½" (3.8 cm)
7 (7, 7, 7½, 7½, 7½, 8, 8)"
18 (18, 18, 19, 19, 20.5, 20.5) cm
14 (15, 15, 15, 15½, 15½, 15½, 15½)"
35.5 (38, 38, 38, 39.5, 39.5, 39.5, 39.5) cm
front & back
6¼" (16 cm)
3½" (9 cm)
6 (6½, 6½, 6¾, 6¾, 7, 7, 7½)"
15 (16.5, 16.5, 17, 17, 18, 18, 19) cm
hips: 25¼ (26½, 26½, 27½, 27½, 28½, 28½, 29½)"
64 (67.5, 67.5, 69, 69, 72.5, 72.5, 75) cm
waist: 15 (16¼, 16¼, 17¼, 18½, 19, 20¼, 21¼)"
38 (41.5, 41.5, 44, 47, 48.5, 51.5, 54) cm
bust: 16¼ (17, 18, 19, 20¼, 21, 22, 23)"
41.5 (43, 45.5, 48.5, 51.5, 53.5, 56, 58,5) cm
12¾ (13, 13½, 13¾, 14½, 15, 15½, 16)"
32.5 (33, 34.5, 35, 37, 38, 39.5, 40.5) cm
3" (7.5 cm)
4¾ (4¾, 4¾, 5, 5¼, 5¼, 5½, 5½)"
12 (12, 12, 12.5, 13.5, 13.5, 14, 14) cm
16 (17, 18, 18, 18, 18, 18, 18)"
40.5 (43, 45.5, 45.5, 45.5, 45.5, 45.5, 45.5) cm
sleeve
4¾" (12 cm)
4½" (11.5 cm)
2½" (6.5 cm)
cuff edge: 11½" (29 cm)
8" (20.5 cm)

Work dec row 0 (0, 0, 0, 1, 0, 1, 1) more time—16 (16, 16, 16, 10, 12, 6, 6) sts total dec'd at side edge; 83 (89, 89, 95, 101, 105, 111, 117) sts rem after gore pleat and side shaping is complete.

Work even until piece measures 9" (23 cm) from CO.

Inc row: K1, M1L (see Glossary), knit to last st, M1R (see Glossary), k1—2 sts inc'd.

Work 7 (9, 5, 5, 5, 5, 5, 5) rows even. Rep the last 8 (10, 6, 6, 6, 6, 6, 6) rows 2 (1, 4, 4, 4, 4, 4, 4) more time(s)—89 (93, 99, 105, 111, 115, 121, 127) sts.

Work even until piece measures 14 (15, 15, 15, 15½, 15½, 15½, 15½)" (35.5 [38, 38, 38, 39.5, 39.5, 39.5, 39.5] cm) from CO, ending with a WS row.

Shape Armholes

BO 4 sts at beg of next 0 (0, 2, 2, 2, 2, 2, 2) rows, then BO 3 sts at beg of foll 2 rows, then BO 2 sts at beg of foll 2 (2, 2, 4, 4, 6, 8, 6) rows—79 (83, 81, 83, 89, 89, 91, 101) sts rem.

Dec row: (RS) K1, k2tog, work to last 3 sts, ssk, k1—2 sts dec'd.

Work 1 WS row even. Rep the last 2 rows 2 (3, 1, 1, 2, 1, 1, 4) more time(s)—73 (75, 77, 79, 83, 85, 87, 91) sts rem.

Work even in St st until armholes measure 7 (7, 7, 7½, 7½, 7½, 8, 8)" (18 [18, 18, 19, 19, 19, 20.5, 20.5] cm).

Place sts on waste-yarn holder.

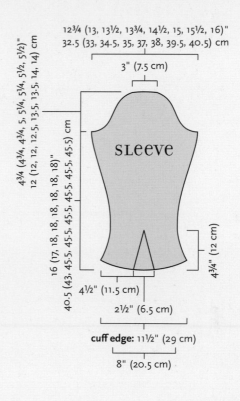

Front

CO and work as for back until piece measures 14 (15, 15, 15, 15½, 15½, 15½, 15½)" (35.5 [38, 38, 38, 39.5, 39.5, 39.5, 39.5] cm) from CO, ending with a WS row—89 (93, 99, 105, 111, 115, 121, 127) sts.

Shape Armholes and Neck

NOTE: Neck shaping is introduced while armhole shaping is in progress; read all the way through the following sections before proceeding.

Place open-ring marker on center st to denote placement of V-neck shaping.

To shape armholes, BO at each armhole edge as foll: 4 sts at beg of next 0 (0, 1, 1, 1, 1, 1, 1) row, then BO 3 sts one time, then BO 2 sts 1 (1, 1, 2, 2, 3, 4, 3) times—5 (5, 9, 11, 11, 13, 15, 15) sts BO at each armhole.

SIZES 32 (34, 36, 38, 40)" ONLY
Dec row: (RS) K1, k2tog, work to last 3 sts, ssk, k1—2 sts dec'd.

Work 1 WS row even.

ALL SIZES
Cont to dec after dividing for neck as foll:

Left front dec row: (RS) K1, k2tog, work to end—1 st dec'd.

Right front dec row: (RS) work to last 3 sts, ssk, k1—1 st dec'd.

Work 1 WS row even.

Rep the last 2 rows 1 (2, 0, 0, 1, 1, 1, 4) more time(s) to complete armhole shaping—3 (4, 2, 2, 3, 2, 2, 5) more sts dec'd at each armhole.

At the same time work the center front even for 5 rows, then cont as foll:

Row 1: (WS) Purl to 1 st before marked center st, pm, p1, p2tog removing m (center st dec'd) and pm after dec, purl to end—1 st dec'd.

Row 2: (RS) Working armhole shaping as established, knit to m, sl m, work button st over next 2 sts, sl m, work to end.

Row 3: Purl to m, sl m, k2, sl m, purl to end.

Row 4: Work to 2 sts before m, 1/1RCP (see Stitch Guide), sl m, p2, sl m, 1/1LCP (see Stitch Guide), work to end.

Row 5: Purl to 2 sts before m, p1, k1, sl m, k2 (center sts), sl m, k1, p1, purl to end.

Row 6: (dividing row) Work to 1 st before m, pm, use the backward-loop method to CO 1 st, remove m, p2—1 st inc'd on left front ; place rem sts on holder to work later for right front.

LEFT FRONT

NOTES: The yoke is worked in St st, while the collar is worked in rev St st. In the following sequence, 2 sts are crossed every 4 rows 6 times, then every other row 7 times. *At the same time*, on alternating RS 4-row repeats, use the backward-loop method (see Glossary) to inc 1 st at neck edge (these inc'd sts will be incorporated into the rev St st collar) as foll:

Row 1: (WS) K3 (collar sts), pm, purl to end.

Row 2: Knit to 2 sts before marker, 1/1RCP, pm between 2 sts of 1/1RCP, purl to end—1 collar st added.

Row 3: knit to m, sl m, purl to end.

Row 4: Knit to m, sl m, use the backward-loop method to CO 1 st, purl to end—1 collar st st inc'd.

Row 5: Knit to m, sl m, purl to end.

Rep Rows 2–5 four more times, then rep Rows 2 and 3 once more, incorporating the purl of the crossed sts and the inc'd sts into the rev St st collar—14 rev St st collar sts.

Next row: (RS) Knit to 2 sts before marker, 1/1RCP, pm between 2 sts of 1/1RCP, use the backward loop method to CO 1 st, purl to end—1 st inc'd; 2 collar sts added total.

Next row: Knit to m, sl m, purl to end.

Next row: Knit to 2 sts before marker, 1/1RCP, pm between 2 sts of 1/1RCP, purl to end.

Next row: Knit to m, sl m, purl to end.

Rep the last 4 rows once more, then rep the last 2 rows once again—44 (45, 46, 47, 49, 50, 51, 53) sts rem: 21 rev St st collar sts; 23 (24, 25, 26, 28, 29, 30, 32) St st yoke sts.

Work even as established until armhole measures 7 (7, 7, 7½, 7½, 7½, 8, 8)" (18 [18, 18, 19, 19, 19, 20.5, 20.5] cm). Place 21 collar sts onto waste yarn; place rem yoke sts on another holder.

RIGHT FRONT
Place held right yoke sts onto needle. With RS facing, join yarn to neck edge.

Row 1: (RS) P2 (collar sts), use the backward-loop method to CO 1 st, pm, knit to end—1 collar st inc'd.

Row 2: (WS) Purl to m, sl m, knit to end.

Row 3: Purl to m, remove m, 1/1LCP (see Stitch Guide), pm between 2 sts of 1/1LCP, knit to end—1 collar st added.

Row 4: Purl to m, sl m, knit to end.

Row 5: Purl to m, use the backward-loop method to CO 1 st, sl m, knit to end—1 collar st inc'd.

Rep Rows 2–5 four more times, then rep Rows 2–4 once more, incorporating the purl of the crossed sts and the inc'd sts into the rev St st collar—14 rev St st collar sts.

Next row: (RS) Purl to m, use the backward-loop method to CO 1 st, remove m, 1/1LCP, pm between 2 sts of 1/1LCP, knit to end—2 collar sts added.

Next row: Purl to m, sl m, knit to end.

Next row: Purl to m, remove m, 1/1LCP, pm between 2 sts of 1/1LCP, knit to end.

Next row: Purl to m, sl m, knit to end.

Rep the last 4 rows once more, then rep the last 2 rows once again—44 (45, 46, 47, 49, 50, 51, 53) sts rem: 21 rev St st collar sts, 23 (24, 25, 26, 28, 29, 30, 32) St st yoke sts.

Work even as established until armhole measures 7 (7, 7, 7½, 7½, 7½, 8, 8)" (18 [18, 18, 19, 19, 19, 20.5, 20.5] cm).

Place 21 collar sts onto waste yarn—23 (24, 25, 26, 28, 29, 30, 32) yoke sts rem on needle. Do not cut yarn.

JOIN SHOULDERS AND EXTEND COLLAR

Place held back sts onto one needle and hold this needle parallel to the needle holding 23 (24, 25, 26, 28, 29, 30, 32) right front sts so that RS of fabric face tog. Use the three-needle method (see Glossary) to BO 23 (24, 25, 26, 28, 29, 30, 32) sts from each needle tog for right shoulder. K27 back neck sts singly, then BO rem 23 (24, 25, 26, 28, 29, 30, 32) back sts tog with held left front sts for left shoulder.

Place each set of 21 collar sts onto same needle holding 27 back neck sts—69 sts total.

Set-up row: (WS) [P1, k1] 12 times, p1, pm, k14, pm, [p1, k1] 12 times, p1.

Row 1: K25, sl m, p14, sl m, knit to end.

Row 2: P25, pm, k14, pm, purl to end.

Rep the last 2 rows once more.

Shape Gore Pleat

NOTE: Bell sleeve is tapered at the same time as gore pleat is worked; read all the way through the following section before proceeding.

Next row: (RS) *Knit to m, sl m, p2tog, purl to 2 sts before next m, ssp (see Glossary), sl m, knit to end—2 sts dec'd.

Work 3 rows even as established. Rep the last 4 rows 5 more times—12 sts dec'd; 2 purl sts rem at top of gore pleat.

Next row: (RS) Knit to 1 st before first m, pm, ssk (removing m to work the dec), k2tog (removing m to work the dec), pm, knit to end—2 sts dec'd; 2 sts between markers.

Purl 1 WS row.

Next row: (RS) Knit to m, sl m, work button st over next 2 sts, sl m, knit to end.

At the same time work 8 rows past the set-up row, then shape sides as foll:

Dec row: (RS) K1, ssk, work row with pleat shaping to last 3 sts, k2tog, k1—2 sts dec'd.

Work 7 rows even. Rep the last 8 rows 2 more times—6 sts total dec'd at side edges; 44 sts rem after all gore pleat and bell shaping is complete.

Work even until piece measures 5" (12.5 cm) from CO, ending with a WS row.

Inc row: (RS) K1, M1L, knit to last 2 sts, M1R, k1—2 sts inc'd.

Cont for your size as foll:

SIZES 32 (34, 36) ONLY
Work 5 rows even. Rep the last 6 rows 12 (13, 14) more times—70 (72, 74) sts.

With yarn still attached to right front, cont as foll:

Row 1: (WS of collar) P21, [k1, p1] 13 times, k1, p21.

Row 2: (RS) K21, [p1, k1] 13 times, p1, k21.

Rep these 2 rows until collar measures 1½" (3.8 cm), ending with a WS row.

With RS facing, BO 21 sts knitwise, then BO 27 in rib patt, then BO rem 21 sts knitwise.

SLEEVES

With CC, CO 64 sts for all sizes. Change to MC and knit 1 RS row.

Dec 1 st each end of needle in this manner every RS row 10 (10, 10, 11, 11, 11, 11, 11) more times—32 (32, 34, 34, 38, 38, 38, 40) sts rem.

BO 2 sts at beg of next 2 (2, 2, 2, 2, 2, 2, 0) rows, then BO 3 sts at beg of foll 4 (4, 2, 2, 6, 6, 6, 8) rows, then BO 4 sts at beg of foll 0 (0, 2, 2, 0, 0, 0, 0) rows—16 sts rem.

BO all sts.

FINISHING

Use the wet-towel method (see Glossary) to block all pieces to measurements, allowing collar to lay flat at back neck and encouraging the V-neck to roll at fronts. Allow to air-dry thoroughly before moving.

Seams

With yarn threaded on a tapestry needle, use the mattress st with ½ st seam allowance (see Glossary) to sew side and sleeve seams. Lightly steam seams from WS to set sts.

Pin sleeve cap into armhole, matching side and sleeve seams, matching center sleeve to shoulder seam and easing fullness at sleeve top. With crochet hook and working from the body side of the seam, use slip-st crochet (see Glossary) to join sleeve to body. Lightly steam armhole seams to set sts.

Weave in loose ends. Lightly steam seams from WS, and finger-press to reduce any bulk.

SIZES (38, 40) ONLY

[Work 5 rows even, rep inc row, then work 3 rows even, rep inc row] 7 (8 times), work 5 rows even, rep inc row once more—(76, 80) sts.

SIZES (42, 44, 46) ONLY

Work 3 rows even. Rep the last 4 rows 18 (20, 21) more times—(82, 86, 88) sts.

ALL SIZES

Work even until sleeve measures 16 (17, 18, 18, 18, 18, 18, 18)" (40.5 [43, 45.5, 45.5, 45.5, 45.5, 45.5, 45.5] cm) from CO, ending with a WS row.

Shape Cap

BO 4 sts at beg of next 0 (2, 2, 2, 2, 2, 2, 2) rows, then BO 3 sts at beg of foll 4 (2, 2, 2, 4, 4, 4) rows, then BO 2 sts at beg of foll 2 (2, 2, 2, 0, 2, 2) rows— 54 (54, 56, 58, 62, 62, 62, 64) sts rem.

Dec row: (RS) K1, k2tog, knit to last 3 sts, ssk, k1— 2 sts dec'd.

RUFFLE SHELL

FINISHED SIZE
About 33 (35, 37, 39, 41, 43)" (84 [89, 94, 99, 104, 109] cm) bust circumference.
Shell shown measures 35" (89 cm).

YARN
DK weight (#3 Light).
Shown here: Skacel Schulana Nocita (78% cotton, 22% nylon; 125 yd [115 m]/50 g): #13 ivory, 6 (6, 7, 7, 8, 8) balls.

NEEDLES
Body: size U.S. 8 (5 mm): 24" (60 cm) circular (cir).
Edging: size U.S. 7 (4.5 mm): 16" (40 cm) cir.
Ruffle: size U.S. 9 (5.5 mm) straight or cir.
Adjust needle size if necessary to obtain the correct gauge.

NOTIONS
Waste yarn for holding sts; tapestry needle.

GAUGE
20 sts and 28 rows = 4" (10 cm) in St st on larger needle.

Softness meets sophistication in this asymmetrically ruffled shell with angled armholes that reveal shapely shoulders. Worked in a tape yarn that combines both matte and shiny threads, this mostly-stockinette-stitch blouse is accented with a bit of openwork rib at the lower edge and a generous garter-stitch ruffle (worked separately and shaped with short-rows). This versatile top can run the gamut between sporty and classic—pair it with a pencil skirt for the executive office, then with a pair of distressed jeans for a night at the movies.

BACK

With smallest needle, CO 86 (92, 98, 102, 106, 112) sts. Do not join for working in rnds.

Eyelet row: (WS) P1, *yo, p2tog; rep from * to last st, yo, p1—87 (93, 99, 103, 107, 113) sts.

Row 1: *K1, p1; rep from * to last st, k1.

Row 2: *P1, k1; rep from * to last st, p1.

Rep Rows 1 and 2 once more.

Change to middle-size needle and work even in St st (knit RS rows; purl WS rows) until piece measures 3 (3, 3½, 3½, 4, 4)" (7.5 [7.5, 9, 9, 10, 10] cm) from CO, ending with a WS row.

Dec row: (RS) K1, k2tog, knit to last 3 sts, ssk, k1—2 sts dec'd.

Work 5 rows even.

Rep the last 6 rows 4 more times—77 (83, 89, 93, 97, 103) sts rem.

Work even until piece measures 9 (9, 9½, 9½, 9½, 9½)" (23 [23, 24, 24, 24, 24] cm) from CO, ending with a WS row.

Inc row: (RS) K1, work left lifted inc (LLI; see Glossary) in next st, knit to last 2 sts, work right lifted inc (RLI; see Glossary) in next st, k1—2 sts inc'd.

Work even until piece measures 11 (11, 11½, 11½, 12, 12)" (28 [28, 29, 29, 30.5, 30.5] cm) from CO, ending with a WS row.

Rep inc row—81 (87, 93, 97, 101, 107) sts.

Work even until piece measures 13½ (13½, 14, 14½, 15, 16)" (34.5 [34.5, 35.5, 37, 38, 40.5] cm) from CO, ending with a WS row.

Shape Armholes

NOTE: Neck shaping is introduced while armhole shaping is in progress; read all the way through the following sections before proceeding.

BO 4 (4, 5, 5, 5, 6) sts at beg of next 2 rows, then BO 3 (3, 3, 3, 3, 4) sts at beg of foll 2 rows, then BO 2 (2, 2, 3, 3, 3) sts at beg of foll 2 rows—63 (69, 73, 75, 79, 81) sts rem.

Dec row: (RS) K1, k2tog, knit to last 3 sts, ssk, k1—2 sts dec'd.

Work 3 rows even.

Rep the last 4 rows 2 (3, 3, 3, 4, 4) more times.

[Rep dec row, then work 5 rows even] 4 (4, 5, 5, 5, 5) times—49 (53, 55, 57, 59, 61) sts rem.

Cont even until armholes measure 6 (6, 6½, 6½, 7, 7)" (15 [15, 16.5, 16.5, 18, 18] cm).

Shape Neck

Mark center 21 (21, 21, 21, 23, 23) sts.

With RS facing and cont to work armhole shaping as established, knit to marked sts, join new yarn and BO center 21 (21, 21, 21, 23, 23) sts, knit to end—14 (16, 17, 18, 18, 19) sts rem each side.

Working each side separately, BO 7 (7, 8, 8, 8, 8) sts at each neck edge once—7 (9, 9, 10, 10, 11) sts rem each side.

Work even until armholes measure 7 (7, 7½, 7½, 8, 8)" (18 [18, 19, 19, 20.5, 20.5] cm), ending with a WS row.

Place sts onto waste yarn holder.

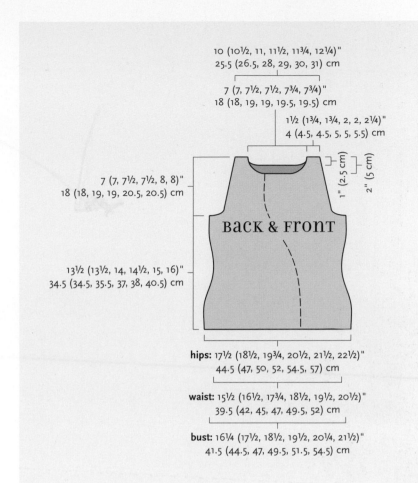

10 (10½, 11, 11½, 11¾, 12¼)"
25.5 (26.5, 28, 29, 30, 31) cm

7 (7, 7½, 7½, 7¾, 7¾)"
18 (18, 19, 19, 19.5, 19.5) cm

1½ (1¾, 1¾, 2, 2, 2¼)"
4 (4.5, 4.5, 5, 5, 5.5) cm

7 (7, 7½, 7½, 8, 8)"
18 (18, 19, 19, 20.5, 20.5) cm

1" (2.5 cm)

2" (5 cm)

BACK & FRONT

13½ (13½, 14, 14½, 15, 16)"
34.5 (34.5, 35.5, 37, 38, 40.5) cm

hips: 17½ (18½, 19¾, 20½, 21½, 22½)"
44.5 (47, 50, 52, 54.5, 57) cm

waist: 15½ (16½, 17¾, 18½, 19½, 20½)"
39.5 (42, 45, 47, 49.5, 52) cm

bust: 16¼ (17½, 18½, 19½, 20¼, 21½)"
41.5 (44.5, 47, 49.5, 51.5, 54.5) cm

FRONT

CO and work same as back until piece measures 13½ (13½, 14, 14½, 15, 16)" (34.5 [34.5, 35.5, 37, 38, 40.5] cm) from CO, ending with a WS row.

Shape Armholes

NOTE: Neck shaping is introduced while armhole shaping is in progress; read all the way through the following sections before proceeding.

BO 4 (4, 5, 5, 5, 6) sts at beg of next 2 rows, then BO 3 (3, 3, 3, 3, 4) sts at beg of foll 2 rows, then BO 2 (2, 2, 3, 3, 3) sts at beg of foll 2 rows—63 (69, 73, 75, 79, 81) sts rem.

Work 3 rows even.

Dec row: (RS) K1, k2tog, knit to last 3 sts, ssk, k1—2 sts dec'd.

Rep the last 4 rows 2 (3, 3, 3, 4, 4) more times.

[Rep dec row, then work 5 rows even] 4 (4, 5, 5, 5, 5) times—14 (16, 18, 18, 20, 20) sts dec'd.

At the same time when armholes measure 5 (5, 5½, 5½, 6, 6)" (12.5 [12.5, 14, 14, 15, 15] cm), shape neck as foll.

Shape Neck

Mark center 15 (15, 15, 15, 17, 17) sts.

With RS facing and cont to work armhole shaping as established, knit to marked sts join new yarn and BO center 15 (15, 15, 15, 17, 17) sts, knit to end—17 (19, 20, 21, 21, 22) sts rem each side.

Working each side separately, BO 4 (4, 5, 5, 5, 5) sts at each neck edge once, then BO 2 sts 2 times—9 (11, 11, 12, 12, 13) sts rem.

Row 6: (short-row) With RS facing, sl 1 pwise wyf, k6, wrap next st, turn work so WS is facing, knit to end.

Row 7: (short-row) With RS facing, sl 1 pwise wyf, k9, wrap next st, turn work so WS is facing, knit to end.

Row 8: (short-row) With RS facing, sl 1 pwise wyf, k12, wrap next st, turn work so WS is facing, knit to end.

Row 9: Rep Row 7.

Row 10: Rep Row 6.

Row 11: Rep Row 5.

Rep Rows 1–11 until piece measures about 20 (20, 21, 22, 23, 24)" (51 [51, 53.5, 56, 58.5, 61] cm) from CO, measured along non-ruffle edge, ending with WS Row 2.

Beg at the ruffle edge, BO all sts.

FINISHING

Use the wet-towel method (see Glossary) to block pieces to measurements. Allow to air-dry completely before moving.

Seams

Place 7 (9, 9, 10, 10, 11) held right back sts onto one needle and 7 (9, 9, 10, 10, 11) held right front sts onto another needle. Hold needles parallel with RS of fabric facing tog and use the three-needle method (see Glossary) to BO sts tog for right shoulder. Rep for left shoulder.

With yarn threaded on a tapestry needle, use the mattress st with ½ st seam allowance (see Glossary) to sew side seams.

Armbands

With smallest cir needle, RS facing, and beg at base of armhole, pick up and knit 40 (41, 42, 43, 45, 47) sts evenly spaced to shoulder seam and 40 (41, 42, 43, 45, 47) sts back down to base of armhole—80 (82, 84, 86, 90, 94) sts total.

Place marker (pm) and join for working in rnds.

Purl 1 rnd, then knit 1 rnd.

BO all sts pwise.

Dec row: (RS) For left neck edge, knit to last 3 sts, ssk, k1; for right neck: k1, k2tog, knit to end.

Purl 1 WS row. Rep dec row once more —7 (9, 9, 10, 10, 11) sts rem each side.

Work even until armholes measure 7 (7, 7½, 7½, 8, 8)" (18 [18, 19, 19, 20.5, 20.5] cm), ending with a WS row.

Place sts onto waste-yarn holder.

RUFFLE

With largest needle, CO 17 sts. Knit 1 row.

Work a series of short-row (see Glossary) triangles on one edge as foll:

Rows 1 and 3: Sl 1 pwise with yarn in front (wyf), knit to end.

Rows 2 and 4: Knit.

Row 5: (short-row) With RS facing, sl 1 pwise wyf, k3, wrap next stitch, turn work so WS is facing, knit to end.

Neckband

With smallest cir needle, RS facing, and beg at left shoulder seam, pick up and knit 43 (43, 45, 45, 47, 47) sts evenly spaced across front neck and 39 (39, 41, 41, 43, 43) sts across back neck—82 (82, 86, 86, 90, 90) sts total.

Pm and join for working in rnds.

Purl 1 rnd, then knit 1 rnd.

BO all sts pwise.

Attach Ruffle

Pin inside edge of ruffle to front as shown in photo, with top of ruffle ¾" (2 cm) from center toward right armhole and forming a gentle S-curve down the front to end at bottom edge about 6 (6, 6½, 6¾, 7, 7½)" (15 [15, 16.5, 17, 18, 19] cm) from left side seam (about one-third of the width of the lower edge).

Thread yarn on a tapestry needle. Insert tapestry needle from WS of garment, leaving a 6" (15 cm) tail. Working from RS of garment, use whipstitches (see Glossary) to capture just the edge of the ruffle in place as invisibly as possible.

Weave in loose ends. Spritz with water to set seams.

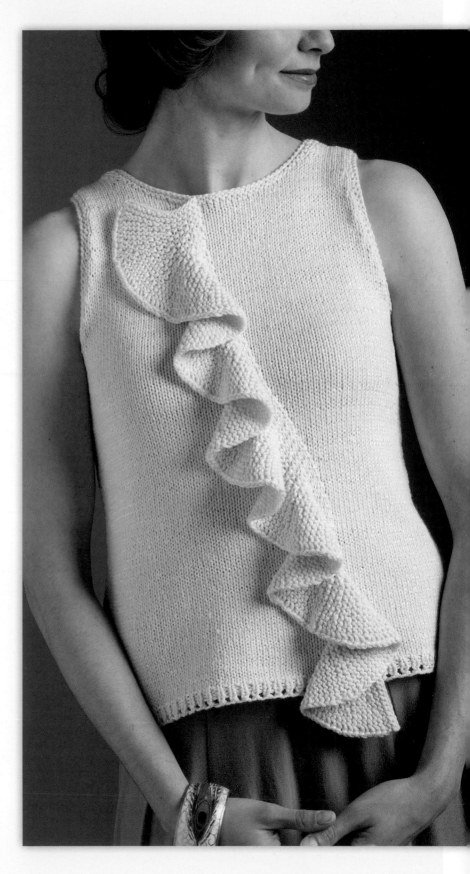

KaLeidoscope

FINISHED SIZE
About 37 (40¼, 44, 47¾)" (94 [102, 112, 121.5] cm) bust circumference, buttoned.
Jacket shown measures 40¼" (102 cm).

YARN
DK weight (#2 Fine).
Shown here: Misti Alpaca (83% Peruvian Pima cotton, 17% silk; 327 yd [300 m]/100 g): CSP12 blue-green handpaint (MC), 4 (5, 5, 6) skeins; TPS03 midnight blue tonal (CC), 1 skein.

NEEDLES
Body and sleeves: size U.S. 6 (4 mm): 24" (60 cm) circular (cir).
Edging: two size U.S. 5 (3.75 mm): 24" (60 cm) cir.
Adjust needle size if necessary to obtain the correct gauge.

NOTIONS
Waste yarn for holding sts; markers (m); size F/5 (3.75 mm) crochet hook; tapestry needle; three 1" (2.5 cm) buttons.

GAUGE
22 sts and 40 rows = 4" (10 cm) in slip st patt on larger needle.
22 st and 27 rows = 4" (10 cm) in St st on larger needle.

With a decidedly ethnic flavor, this slightly A-line jacket features a deep U-neckline, half collar, and minimal button overlap. A slip-stitch texture pattern, worked throughout the body and the sleeve cuffs, showcases the handpainted yarn to best advantage. The edgings and ribbed collar are worked in an accent color that helps to define the parts and unify the whole. With an easy fit, this jacket is ideal for layering over whatever style strikes your fancy: narrow-leg pants, a pencil skirt, camisole, tee shirt, long gauzy skirt, or a little sheath dress.

STITCH GUIDE

Slip-Stitch Pattern (*multiple of 4 sts + 1*)

Row 1: (WS) Purl.

Row 2: (RS) K1, *sl 1 purlwise with yarn in back (pwise wyb), sl 1 purlwise with yarn in front (pwise wyf), sl 1 pwise wyb, k1; rep from *.

Row 3: P1, *sl 3 pwise wyb, yo, p1; rep from *.

Row 4: Knit, dropping all yo's off needle to front of work.

Row 5: Purl.

Row 6: K1, *sl 1 pwise wyb, insert needle from front under the loose strand and knit next st together with this strand, sl 1 pwise wyb, k1; rep from *.

Row 7: P1, *sl 1 pwise wyf, p1, sl 1 pwise wyf, k1; rep from *, ending last rep p1 instead of k1.

Row 8: Knit.

Row 9: Purl.

Row 10: K1, *sl 1 pwise wyf, k1; rep from *.

Rep Rows 1–10 for patt.

BACK

With MC and larger needle, CO 105 (117, 129, 141) sts. Do not join for working in rnds.

Row 1: (WS) *P1, k1; rep from * to last st, p1.

Row 2: *K1, p1; rep from * to last st, k1.

Beg with Row 1 (WS), work even in slip st patt (see Stitch Guide) until piece measures 3" (7.5 cm) from CO, ending with a WS row.

Dec row: K2tog, work in patt to last 2 sts, ssk—2 sts dec'd.

Work even, keeping continuity of patt as much as you can (work extra sts in st st), rep dec row at 6" (15 cm), 9" (23 cm), and 12" (30.5 cm) from CO—97 (109, 121, 133) sts rem.

Cont even until piece meas 15 (15, 16, 17)" (38 [38, 40.5, 43] cm) from CO, ending with a WS row.

Shape Armholes

Keeping in patt, BO 4 sts at beg of next 2 (2, 4, 6) rows—89 (101, 105, 109) sts rem.

Dec 1 st each end of needle every RS row 6 (8, 8, 8) times—77 (85, 89, 93) sts rem.

Work even in patt until armholes measure about 7½ (8, 8, 8½)" (19 [20.5, 20.5, 21.5] cm), ending with any WS row except Row 5 of patt.

Place sts onto waste-yarn holder.

RIGHT FRONT

With MC and larger needle, CO 57 (61, 65, 69) sts. Do not join.

Row 1: (WS) *P1, k1; rep from * to last st, p1.

Row 2: *K1, p1; rep from * to last st, k1.

Beg with Row 1, work even in slip st patt until piece measures 3" (7.5 cm) from CO, ending with a WS row.

Dec row: (RS) Work in patt to last 2 sts, ssk—1 st dec'd.

Keeping in patt as much as possible (work extra sts in St st), rep dec row when piece measures 6" (15 cm), 9" (23 cm), and 12" (30.5 cm) from CO—53 (57, 61, 65) sts rem.

Cont even until piece measures 15 (15, 16, 17)" (38 [38, 40.5, 43] cm) from CO, ending with RS row.

Shape Armhole and Neck

NOTE: Neck shaping is introduced at the same time as armhole shaping is in progress; read all the way through the following sections before proceeding.

At armhole edge (beg of WS rows), BO 4 sts 1 (1, 2, 3) time(s)—49 (53, 53, 53) sts rem.

Dec 1 st at end of every RS row 6 (8, 8, 8) times and *at the same time* when piece measures 17½ (17½, 18½, 19½)" (44.5 [44.5, 47, 49.5] cm) from CO, shape neck as foll:

At neck edge (beg of RS rows), BO 4 sts once, then BO 2 sts 3 (4, 4, 4) times—10 (12, 12, 12) sts BO.

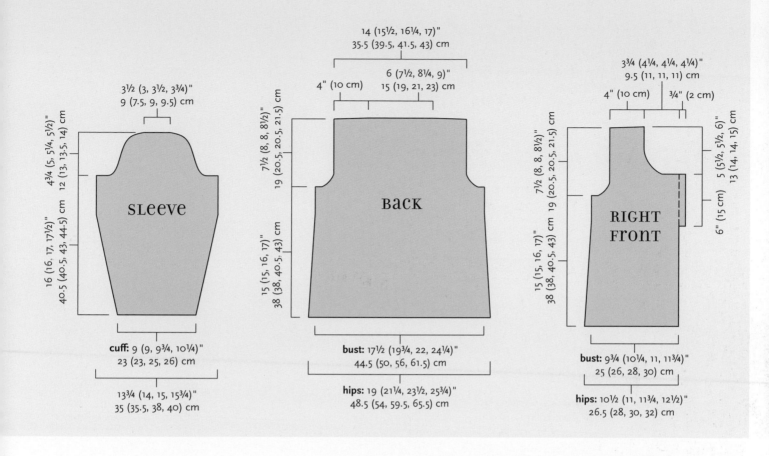

sleeve

3½ (3, 3½, 3¾)"
9 (7.5, 9, 9.5) cm

4¾ (5, 5¼, 5½)"
12 (13, 13.5, 14) cm

16 (16, 17, 17½)"
40.5 (40.5, 43, 44.5) cm

cuff: 9 (9, 9¾, 10¼)"
23 (23, 25, 26) cm

13¾ (14, 15, 15¾)"
35 (35.5, 38, 40) cm

back

14 (15½, 16¼, 17)"
35.5 (39.5, 41.5, 43) cm

4" (10 cm)

6 (7½, 8¼, 9)"
15 (19, 21, 23) cm

7½ (8, 8, 8½)"
19 (20.5, 20.5, 21.5) cm

15 (15, 16, 17)"
38 (38, 40.5, 43) cm

bust: 17½ (19¾, 22, 24¼)"
44.5 (50, 56, 61.5) cm

hips: 19 (21¼, 23½, 25¾)"
48.5 (54, 59.5, 65.5) cm

RIGHT FRONT

3¾ (4¼, 4¼, 4¼)"
9.5 (11, 11, 11) cm

4" (10 cm) ¾" (2 cm)

5 (5½, 5½, 6)"
13 (14, 14, 15) cm

6" (15 cm)

7½ (8, 8, 8½)"
19 (20.5, 20.5, 21.5) cm

15 (15, 16, 17)"
38 (38, 40.5, 43) cm

bust: 9¾ (10¼, 11, 11¾)"
25 (26, 28, 30) cm

hips: 10½ (11, 11¾, 12½)"
26.5 (28, 30, 32) cm

Dec 1 st at neck edge every RS row 11 times—22 sts rem when all armhole and neck decs have been completed.

Work even in patt until armholes measure about 7½ (8, 8, 8½)" (19 [20.5, 20.5, 21.5] cm), ending with any WS row except Row 5 of patt.

Place sts on waste yarn holder.

LEFT FRONT

With MC and larger needle, CO 57 (61, 65, 69) sts. Do not join.

Row 1: (WS) *P1, k1; rep from * to last st, p1.

Row 2: *K1, p1; rep from * to last st, k1.

Beg with Row 1, work even in slip st patt until piece meaures 3" (7.5 cm) from CO, ending with a WS row.

Dec row: (RS) K2tog, work in patt to end—1 st dec'd.

Keeping in patt as much as possible (work extra sts in St st), rep dec row when piece measures 6" (15 cm), 9" (23 cm), and 12" (30.5 cm) from CO—53 (57, 61, 65) sts rem.

Cont even until piece measures 15 (15, 16, 17)" (38 [38, 40.5, 43] cm) from CO, ending with WS row.

Shape Armhole and Neck

NOTE: Neck shaping is introduced at the same time as armhole shaping is in progress; read all the way through the following sections before proceeding.

At armhole edge (beg of RS rows), BO 4 sts 1 (1, 2, 3) time(s)— 49 (53, 53, 53) sts rem.

Dec 1 st at end of every RS row 6 (8, 8, 8) times and *at the same time* when piece measures 17½ (17½, 18½, 19½)" (44.5 [44.5, 47, 49.5] cm) from CO, shape neck as foll:

At neck edge (beg of WS rows), BO 4 sts once, then BO 2 sts 3 (4, 4, 4) times—10 (12, 12, 12) sts BO.

Dec 1 st at neck edge every RS row 11 times—22 sts rem when all armhole and neck decs have been completed.

Work even in patt until armholes measure about 7½ (8, 8, 8½)" (19 [20.5, 20.5, 21.5] cm), ending with any WS row except Row 5 of patt.

Place sts onto waste-yarn holder.

SLEEVES

With MC and larger needle, CO 49 (49, 53, 57) sts. Do not join.

Row 1: (WS) *P1, k1; rep from * to last st, p1.

Row 2: *K1, p1; rep from * to last st, k1.

Work Rows 1–10 of slip st patt 3 times—piece measures about 3" (7.5 cm) from CO.

Purl 1 WS row.

Inc row: (RS) K1, work left lifted inc (LLI; see Glossary) in next st, knit to last 2 sts, work right lifted inc (RLI; see Glossary) in next st, k1—2 sts inc'd.

Work 5 rows even.

Rep the last 6 rows 12 (13, 14, 14) times—75 (77, 83, 87) sts.

Work even until piece measures 16 (16, 17, 17½)" (40.5 [40.5, 43, 44.5] cm) from CO, ending with a WS row.

Shape Cap

BO 4 sts at beg of next 2 rows, then BO 2 sts at beg of foll 10 (10, 12, 12) rows—47 (49, 51, 55) sts rem.

Dec row: (RS) K1, k2tog, knit to last 3 sts, ssk, k1—2 sts dec'd.

Dec 1 st each of needle in this manner every RS row 5 (5, 5, 6) more times—35 (37, 39, 41) sts rem.

BO 2 sts at beg of next 8 (10, 10, 10) rows—19 (17, 19, 21) sts rem.

BO all sts.

FINISHING

Left Front Tab Placket

Mark center left front 6" (15 cm) down from neck edge. With CC, smaller needle, RS facing, and beg at neck edge, pick up and knit 31 sts evenly spaced to marker. Knit 7 rows.

Place sts onto holder.

Right Front Tab Placket

Mark center right front 6" (15 cm) down from neck edge. With CC, smaller needle, RS facing, and beg at marked position, pick up and knit 31 sts evenly spaced to neck edge. Knit 3 rows.

Buttonhole row: (RS) K5, *work 4-st one-row buttonhole (see Glossary), k4 (5 sts on right needle tip after buttonhole); rep from *, ending last rep k3 instead of k4.

Knit 3 rows.

Place sts onto holder.

Wet-block (see Glossary) pieces to measurements. Allow to air-dry completely before moving.

Join Shoulders

Place 77 (85, 89, 93) held back sts onto one needle and 22 held right front sts onto another needle. Hold needles parallel with RS of fabric facing tog. With MC and larger needle, use the three-needle method (see Glossary) to BO 22 sts tog for right shoulder. BO next 33 (41, 45, 49) sts singly for back neck. Place 22 held left front sts onto second needle and use the three-needle method to BO sts tog for left shoulder.

Armbands

Wth CC, smaller needle, and RS facing, pick up and knit 84 (88, 94, 106) sts evenly spaced around armhole. Do not join. Knit 2 rows. BO all sts.

Front Edge Border and Collar

With CC, smaller needle, and beg at lower right front center edge, pick up and knit 60 (60, 65, 70) sts evenly spaced to base of tab, 5 sts across lower edge of tab, 31 sts along vertical edge of tab, 5 sts across top edge of tab, 45 (48, 48, 48) sts along right neck and *at the same time* place a marker after the 20th (23rd, 23rd, 23rd) st, 41 sts across back neck, 45 (48, 48, 48) sts along left neck to tab and *at the same time* place a marker after the 25th st, 5 sts across top edge of tab, 31 sts along vertical edge of tab, 5 sts across lower edge of tab, and 60 (60, 65, 70) sts along left center front—333 (339, 349, 359) sts total.

Use second smaller needle to knit back and forth, using both cir needles to accommodate all sts.

Row 1: (WS) Knit.

Row 2: Knit to inside corner of tab, k2tog, knit to outside corner of tab, M1 (see Glossary), knit to next outside corner, M1, knit to right shoulder seam, knit across back neck and *at the same time* dec 4 sts evenly spaced, knit to next outside corner, M1, knit to next outside corner, M1, knit to inside corner, k2tog, knit to end—331 (337, 347, 357) sts rem.

Row 3: BO to first m, remove m, BO 1 st, knit to next m, remove m, BO to end of row—91 sts rem.

Cut yarn and draw through last loop to secure.

Collar

With RS facing, rejoin CC to live sts at right neck and sl 1 pwise wyb, knit to end.

Cont as foll:

Row 1: (WS) Sl 1 pwise wyf, k1, *p1, k1; rep from * to last st, p1.

Row 2: Sl 1 pwise wyb, p1, *k1, p1; rep from * to last st, k1.

Rows 3 and 4: Rep Rows 1 and 2.

Row 5: Sl 1, ssp (see Glossary), k1, *p1, k1; rep from * to last 3 sts, p2tog, p1—2 sts dec'd.

Rows 6, 7, and 8: Rep Rows 2, 3 and 4.

Row 9: Sl 1, ssk, *p1, k1; rep from * to last 3 sts, k2tog, p1—2 sts dec'd.

Rows 10 and 12: Rep Row 2.

Row 11: Rep Row 5—2 sts dec'd.

Row 13: Rep Row 9—83 sts rem.

Working first and last 2 sts tog, BO all sts in patt.

Seams

With MC threaded on a tapestry needle, use the mattress st with ½ st seam allowance (see Glossary) to sew side and sleeve seams. With MC and a crochet hook, use slip st crochet (see Glossary) to join sleeve cap to armhole, matching side and sleeve seams and matching center sleeve cap to shoulder seam, easing in fullness at cap as necessary and working from the body (not the sleeve) side of the join.

Lightly steam edge border from WS. Do not steam ribbed collar.

Lap right tab placket over left tab so that the lower center front edges just meet, and mark button placement on left tab, opposite buttonholes. Sew buttons in place.

Steam lightly from WS to set sts.

Weave in loose ends.

wrap blouse

FINISHED SIZE
About 34 (36, 38, 40, 42, 44, 46, 48)" (86.5
[91.5, 96.5, 101.5, 106.5, 112, 117, 122] cm)
bust circumference.
Top shown measures 36" (91.5 cm).

YARN
DK weight (#3).

Shown here: South West Trading Bamboo
(100% bamboo; 250 yd [228.5 m]/100 g):
#138 purplexed, 5 (5, 6, 6, 7, 7, 7, 8) balls.

NEEDLES
Body and sleeves: size U.S. 6 (4 mm):
24" (60 cm) circular (cir).
I-cord edging: size U.S. 4 (3.5 mm):
24" (60 cm) cir.
*Adjust needle size if necessary to obtain the
correct gauge.*

NOTIONS
Stitch holders; markers (m); size F/5
(4 mm) crochet hook; tapestry needle;
2⅛" (5.3 cm) diameter buckle (available at
fabric stores).

GAUGE
24 sts and 30 rows = 4" (10 cm) in St st on
larger needle.

Nothing is more effective for flattering and
shaping every body type than a surplice wrap.
The diagonal lines from neck to buckle and
from buckle to hem elongate the silhouette,
while soft pleats offer definition at the waist as
well as a bit of cover-up. The waist and sleeve
cuffs are worked in linen stitch, which provides
welcome stability in this otherwise fluid blouse.
The artistically offset diagonal lower front
edges create sophistication; three-quarter-
length sleeves offer versatile comfort. The
extraordinarily fine drape of the bamboo yarn
is crucial for the success of this design.

Linen Stitch (*even number of sts*)

Row 1: (RS) *K1, sl 1 pwise with yarn in front (wyf); rep from to last 2 sts, k2.

Row 2: (WS) *P1, sl 1 pwise with yarn in back (wyb); rep from * to last 2 sts, p2.

Rep Rows 1 and 2 for patt.

BACK

With larger needle, CO 108 (114, 120, 126, 132, 138, 144, 150) sts. Do not join for working in rnds.

Purl 1 WS row, then work even in St st for 10 rows, ending with a WS row.

Side Decreases

Dec row: (RS) K1, k2tog, knit to last 3 sts, ssk, k1—2 sts dec'd.

Work 7 rows even. Rep the last 8 rows 5 more times—96 (102, 108, 114, 120, 126, 132, 138) sts rem.

Work even until piece measures 8½" (21.5 cm) from CO, ending with a RS row.

Next row: (WS) P7 (8, 8, 9, 9, 10, 10, 11), *p2tog, p14 (15, 16, 17, 18, 19, 20, 21); rep from * 4 more times, p2tog, p7 (7, 8, 8, 9, 9, 10, 10)—90 (96, 102, 108, 114, 120, 126, 132) sts rem.

Work even in linen st (see Stitch Guide) until piece measures 11" (28 cm) from CO, ending with a WS row—linen st "waistband" measures 2½" (6.5 cm).

Next row: (RS) K7 (8, 8, 9, 9, 10, 10, 11), k1f&b (see Glossary), *k14 (15, 16, 17, 18, 19, 20, 21), k1f&b; rep from * 4 more times, k7 (7, 8, 8, 9, 9, 10, 10)—96 (102, 108, 114, 120, 126, 132, 138) sts.

Work 9 rows even in St st, ending with a WS row.

Side Increases

Inc row: (RS) K1, M1L (see Glossary), knit to last st, M1R (see Glossary), k1—2 sts inc'd.

Work 9 rows even in St st. Rep the last 10 rows once, then rep inc row once again—102 (108, 114, 120, 126, 132, 138, 144) sts.

Work even in St until piece measures 17" (43 cm) from CO, ending with a WS row.

Shape Armholes

BO 4 sts at beg of next 2 rows, then BO 3 sts at beg of foll 2 (2, 2, 2, 2, 4, 4, 4) rows, then BO 2 sts at beg of foll 0 (2, 2, 2, 4, 2, 4, 6) rows—88 (90, 96, 102, 104, 108, 110, 112) sts rem.

Dec row: (RS) K1, k2tog, knit to last 3 sts, ssk, k1—2 sts dec'd.

Purl 1 WS row. Rep the last 2 rows 2 (1, 2, 3, 3, 3, 3, 3) more time(s)—82 (86, 90, 94, 96, 100, 102, 104) sts rem.

Work even in St st until armholes measure 7 (7, 7, 7½, 7½, 7½, 8, 8)" (18 [18, 18, 19, 19, 19, 20.5, 20.5] cm), ending with a WS row.

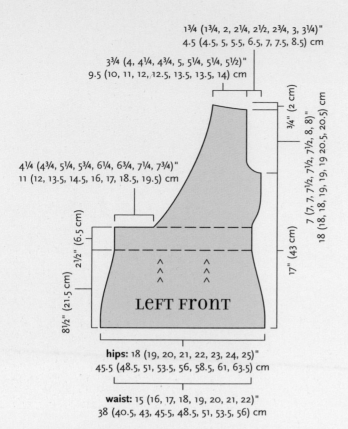

1¾ (1¾, 2, 2¼, 2½, 2¾, 3, 3¼)"
4.5 (4.5, 5, 5.5, 6.5, 7, 7.5, 8.5) cm

3¾ (4, 4¼, 4¾, 5, 5¼, 5¼, 5½)"
9.5 (10, 11, 12, 12.5, 13.5, 13.5, 14) cm

¾" (2 cm)

4¼ (4¾, 5¼, 5¾, 6¼, 6¾, 7¼, 7¾)"
11 (12, 13.5, 14.5, 16, 17, 18.5, 19.5) cm

7 (7, 7, 7½, 7½, 7½, 8, 8)"
18 (18, 18, 19, 19 20.5, 20.5) cm

17" (43 cm)

2½" (6.5 cm)

8½" (21.5 cm)

Left Front

hips: 18 (19, 20, 21, 22, 23, 24, 25)"
45.5 (48.5, 51, 53.5, 56, 58.5, 61, 63.5) cm

waist: 15 (16, 17, 18, 19, 20, 21, 22)"
38 (40.5, 43, 45.5, 48.5, 51, 53.5, 56) cm

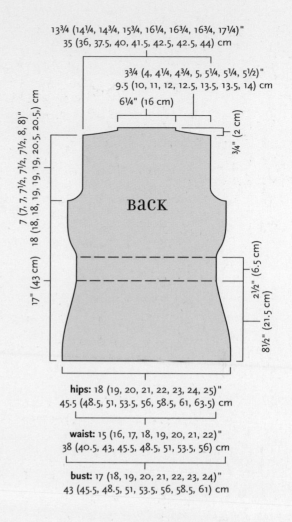

13¾ (14¼, 14¾, 15¾, 16¼, 16¾, 16¾, 17¼)"
35 (36, 37.5, 40, 41.5, 42.5, 42.5, 44) cm

3¾ (4, 4¼, 4¾, 5, 5¼, 5¼, 5½)"
9.5 (10, 11, 12, 12.5, 13.5, 13.5, 14) cm

6¼" (16 cm)

¾" (2 cm)

7 (7, 7, 7½, 7½, 7½, 8, 8)"
18 (18, 18, 19, 19, 20.5, 20.5) cm

back

17" (43 cm)

2½" (6.5 cm)

8½" (21.5 cm)

hips: 18 (19, 20, 21, 22, 23, 24, 25)"
45.5 (48.5, 51, 53.5, 56, 58.5, 61, 63.5) cm

waist: 15 (16, 17, 18, 19, 20, 21, 22)"
38 (40.5, 43, 45.5, 48.5, 51, 53.5, 56) cm

bust: 17 (18, 19, 20, 21, 22, 23, 24)"
43 (45.5, 48.5, 51, 53.5, 56, 58.5, 61) cm

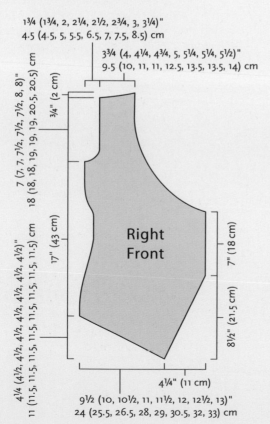

1¾ (1¾, 2, 2¼, 2½, 2¾, 3, 3¼)"
4.5 (4.5, 5, 5.5, 6.5, 7, 7.5, 8.5) cm

3¾ (4, 4¼, 4¾, 5, 5¼, 5¼, 5½)"
9.5 (10, 11, 11, 12.5, 13.5, 13.5, 14) cm

¾" (2 cm)

7 (7, 7, 7½, 7½, 7½, 8, 8)"
18 (18, 18, 19, 19, 20.5, 20.5) cm

17" (43 cm)

7" (18 cm)

8½" (21.5 cm)

Right Front

4¼ (4½, 4½, 4½, 4½, 4½, 4½, 4½)"
11 (11.5, 11.5, 11.5, 11.5, 11.5, 11.5, 11.5) cm

4¼" (11 cm)

9½ (10, 10½, 11, 11½, 12, 12½, 13)"
24 (25.5, 26.5, 28, 29, 30.5, 32, 33) cm

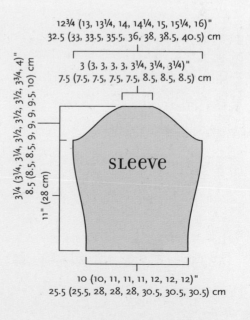

12¾ (13, 13¼, 14, 14¼, 15, 15¼, 16)"
32.5 (33, 33.5, 35.5, 36, 38, 38.5, 40.5) cm

3 (3, 3, 3, 3, 3¼, 3¼, 3¼)"
7.5 (7.5, 7.5, 7.5, 7.5, 8.5, 8.5, 8.5) cm

3¼ (3¼, 3¼, 3½, 3½, 3½, 3¾, 4)"
8.5 (8.5, 8.5, 9, 9, 9, 9.5, 10) cm

11" (28 cm)

sleeve

10 (10, 11, 11, 11, 12, 12, 12)"
25.5 (25.5, 28, 28, 28, 30.5, 30.5, 30.5) cm

Shape Shoulders

Work short-rows (see Glossary) as foll:

Short-Row 1: With RS facing, knit to last 11 (12, 13, 14, 15, 16, 16, 16) sts, wrap next st, turn work so WS is facing, purl to last 11 (12, 13, 14, 15, 16, 16, 16) sts, wrap next st, turn work.

Short-Row 2: With RS facing, knit to last 22 (24, 26, 28, 29, 31, 32, 33) sts, wrap next st, turn work so WS is facing, purl to last 22 (24, 26, 28, 29, 31, 32, 33) sts, wrap next st, turn work.

Next row: With RS facing, knit to end, working wraps tog with wrapped sts when you come to them.

Next row: With WS facing, purl to end, working wraps tog with wrapped sts when you come to them.

Place sts on holder.

under-peplum and left front

....

NOTE: Waist darts and armhole shaping are introduced at the same time as side shaping is in progress; read all the way through the following sections before proceeding.

....

With larger needle, CO 108 (114, 120, 126, 132, 138, 144, 150) sts. Do not join.

Purl 1 WS row, then work even in St st for 10 rows.

Side and Dart Decreases

Dec row: (RS) K1, k2tog, knit to last 3 sts, ssk, k1—2 sts dec'd.

Work 7 rows even. Rep the last 8 rows 5 times and *at the same time* when piece measures 5½" (14 cm) from CO, work waist darts as foll:

Mark center 30 (32, 34, 36, 36, 38, 40, 42) sts for dart placement.

Dart dec row: Knit to first m, slip marker (sl m), ssk, knit to 2 sts before second m, k2tog, sl m, knit to end—2 sts dec'd.

Working side shaping as established, rep dart dec row when piece measures 6½" (16.5 cm) and again when piece measures 7½" (19 cm) from CO—90 (96, 102, 108, 114, 120, 126, 132) sts rem when all dart shaping is complete.

Cont working side shaping as established until piece measures 8½" (21.5 cm) from CO, ending with a RS row.

Work even in linen st until piece measures 11" (28 cm) from CO, ending with a RS row—linen st "waistband" measures 2½" (6.5 cm).

Next row: (WS) Cont in linen st, BO 26 (29, 32, 35, 38, 41, 44, 47) sts, then work to end—64 (67, 70, 73, 76, 79, 82, 85) sts rem.

Shape Neck

Dec row: (RS) Knit to last 3 sts, ssk, k1—1 st dec'd.

Rep dec row every RS row 24 more times, then every 4th row 10 times—35 sts dec'd at neck edge.

At the same time when piece measures 12" (30.5 cm) from CO, shape the side edge as foll.

Side Increases

Inc row: (RS) K1, M1L, knit to end—1 st inc'd.

Work 9 rows even at side edge. Rep the last 10 rows once, then rep inc row once again—3 sts inc'd at side edge.

At the same time when piece measures 17" (43 cm) from CO (bodice measures 6" [15 cm] from top of waistband), shape armholes as foll.

Shape Armholes

Working neck and side shaping as established, at armhole edge (beg of RS rows), BO 4 sts once, then BO 3 sts 1 (1, 1, 1, 2, 2, 2) time(s), then BO 2 sts 0 (1, 1, 1, 2, 1, 2, 3) time(s)—7 (9, 9, 9, 11, 12, 14, 16) sts BO.

Dec row: (RS) K1, k2tog, knit to end—1 st dec'd.

Work 1 WS row even. Rep the last 2 rows 2 (1, 2, 3, 3, 3, 3, 3) more time(s) to complete armhole shaping—22 (24, 26, 28, 29, 31, 32, 33) sts rem for each shoulder when all side, neck, and armhole shaping is complete.

Work even until armhole measures 7 (7, 7, 7½, 7½, 7½, 8, 8)" (18 [18, 18, 19, 19, 19, 20.5, 20.5] cm), ending with a RS row.

Shape Shoulder

Short-Row 1: With WS facing, p11 (12, 13, 14, 14, 15, 16, 17), wrap next st, turn work so RS is facing, k11 (12, 13, 14, 14, 15, 16, 17), turn work.

Next row: (WS) Purl, working wrap tog with wrapped st when you come to it.

Place sts on holder.

RIGHT Front

CO 2 sts. Purl 1 (WS) row.

Shape center front (right edge) as foll.

RS Inc row: K1, M1, knit to end—1 st inc'd.

[Work 1 row even, rep inc row; then work 3 rows even, rep inc row] 10 times.

WS Inc row: Purl to last st, M1 pwise, p1—1 st inc'd.

Rep RS Inc row, then rep WS inc row—24 sts inc'd.

At the same time shape lower edge for your size as folls:

Knit to end of row (left edge), turn work so WS is facing, then use the cable method (see Glossary) to CO the specified number of sts for your size, then purl to end as foll.

SIZES 34 (36, 38, 40)" ONLY

[CO 4 sts, then CO 3 sts] 7 (8, 8, 7) times, then CO 4 (4, 7, 5) sts 2 (1, 1, 2) time(s), then CO 7 sts 0 (0, 0, 1) time—57 (60, 63, 66) sts CO.

SIZES 42 (44)" ONLY

[CO 4 sts] 16 (15) times, then CO 5 (6) sts 1 (2) time(s)—69 (72) sts CO.

SIZES 46 (48)" ONLY

[CO 5 sts, then CO 4 sts] 8 times, then CO 3 (6) sts once—75 (78) sts CO.

At the same time when lower edge shaping is complete, work even at side edge for 10 rows while cont to inc on center front edge.

Side Decreases

Dec row: (RS) Work to last 3 sts, ssk, k1—1 st dec'd.

Work 7 rows even at side edge. Rep the last 8 rows 5 more times—6 sts dec'd at side edge.

Cont even on all sts until piece measures 7" (18 cm) from last center front inc.

Shape Neck

NOTE: For a smooth BO edge, use the sloped method (see Glossary) to BO along the neck edge.

At neck edge (beg of RS rows), BO 5 sts once, then BO 4 sts 3 times, then BO 2 sts 3 times—23 sts BO.

Dec row: (RS) K1, k2tog, knit to end—1 st dec'd.

Dec 1 st at neck edge in this manner every RS row 14 more times, then every 4th row 10 times—25 sts dec'd total.

Side Increases

At the same time, when piece measures 12½" (31.5 cm) at side edge, inc as foll:

Inc row: (RS) Knit to last st, M1R, k1—1 st inc'd.

Work 9 rows even at side edge. Rep the last 10 rows once, then rep inc row once more—3 sts inc'd at side edge.

Also at the same time, when piece meaures 17" (43 cm) from CO at side edge shape armhole as foll.

Shape Armhole

Working neck shaping as established, at armhole edge (beg of WS rows), BO 4 sts once, then BO 3 sts 1 (1, 1, 1, 1, 2, 2, 2) time(s), then BO 2 sts 0 (1, 1, 1, 2, 1, 2, 3) time(s)—7 (9, 9, 9, 11, 12, 14, 16) sts BO.

Dec row: (RS) Work to last 3 sts, ssk, k1—1 st dec'd.

Work 1 WS row even. Rep the last 2 rows 2 (1, 2, 3, 3, 3, 3, 3) more time(s) to complete armhole shaping—3 (2, 3, 4, 4, 4, 4, 4) sts dec'd; 22 (24, 26, 28, 29, 31, 32, 33) sts rem when all shaping is complete.

Cont neck shaping as established, work armhole edge even until armhole measures 7 (7, 7, 7½, 7½, 7½, 8, 8)" (18 [18, 18, 19, 19, 19, 20.5, 20.5] cm), ending with a RS row.

Shape Shoulder

Short-Row 1: With RS facing, k11 (12, 13, 14, 14, 15, 16, 17), wrap next st, turn work so WS is facing, p11 (12, 13, 14, 14, 15, 16, 17).

Next row: (RS) Knit, working wrap tog with wrapped st when you come to it.

Place sts on holder.

SLEEVES

With larger needle, CO 60 (60, 66, 66, 66, 72, 72, 72) sts. Do not join.

Work in linen st until piece measures 1½" (3.8 cm) from CO, ending with a WS row.

Inc row: (RS) K1, M1L, knit to last st, M1R, k1—2 sts inc'd.

Work 7 (7, 9, 7, 5, 7, 5, 5) rows even. Rep the last 8 (8, 10, 8, 6, 8, 6, 6) rows 7 (8, 6, 8, 9, 8, 9, 11) more times—76 (78, 80, 84, 86, 90, 92, 96) sts.

Work even until piece measures 11" (28 cm) from CO, ending with a WS row.

Shape Cap

BO 4 sts at beg of next 2 rows, then BO 3 sts at beg of foll 2 (2, 4, 4, 4, 6, 6, 6) rows, then BO 2 sts at beg of foll 2 (2, 0, 2, 2, 0, 0, 2) rows—58 (60, 60, 60, 62, 64, 66, 66) sts rem.

Dec row: (RS) K1, k2tog, knit to last 3 sts, ssk, k1—2 sts dec'd.

Dec 1 st each end of needle in this manner every RS row 13 (13, 13, 13, 14, 14, 15, 15) more times—30 (32, 32, 32, 32, 34, 34, 34) sts rem.

BO 3 sts at beg of next 4 (2, 2, 2, 2, 2, 2) rows, then BO 4 sts at beg of foll 0 (2, 2, 2, 2, 2, 2, 2) rows—18 (18, 18, 18, 18, 20, 20, 20) sts rem.

BO all sts.

FINISHING

Blocking

Steam-block (see Glossary) all pieces to measurements, pressing lightly to encourage lower edge lie flat. Steam from both RS and WS. Let air-dry thoroughly before moving.

Join Shoulders

Place 82 (86, 90, 94, 96, 100, 102, 104) back sts onto one needle and 22 (24, 26, 28, 29, 31, 32, 33) right front sts and 22 (24, 26, 28, 29, 31, 32, 33) left front sts onto another needle. Hold needles parallel with RS of fabric facing tog and use the three-needle method (see Glossary) to BO right front sts tog with back sts for right shoulder. BO next 38 back sts singly for back neck, then BO rem back sts tog with left front sts for left shoulder.

Seams

With yarn threaded on a tapestry needle, use the mattress st with ½-st seam allowance (see Glossary) to sew side seams.

With WS of garment facing, pin left front at the right side seam, aligning linen st waistband and lower edges. With yarn threaded on a tapestry needle, whipstitch (see Glossary) left front edge to right seam allowance.

Using the mattress st with ½-st seam allowance, sew sleeve seams. Lightly steam seams from WS.

Pin sleeve cap into armhole, matching side and sleeve seams and matching center sleeve cap to shoulder seam, easing fullness at sleeve top. With crochet hook and working from the body side of the seam, use slip-st crochet (see Glossary) to join sleeve to body. Lightly steam-block armhole seams.

Right Front Pleats

Mark the upper corner and the lower corner of the left 7" (18 cm) edge of right front. Make four pleat folds, each ½" (1.3 cm) wide with fold edges facing down as shown at lower right—2½" (6.5 cm) rem between markers.

With crochet hook and RS facing, work about 15 single crochet (sc; see Glossary) sts between markers, inserting hook through all three layers of each fold to secure. Pull entire ball through last loop to secure.

With attached working yarn and smaller cir needle, pick up and knit 1 st for each st along BO edges and about 3 sts for every 4 rows along dec shaping—about 90 (90, 90, 93, 93, 93, 96, 96) sts along right front edge, 38 sts across back neck, and 83 (83, 83, 86, 86, 86, 89, 89) sts along left front edge. Cut yarn, leaving an 8" (20.5 cm) tail to weave in.

Return to the first picked up st and use the cable method (see Glossary) to CO 2 more sts.

Work I-cord BO as foll: With RS facing, *k1, ssk (1 I-cord st and 1 body st), return these 2 sts onto left needle tip, pull yarn tightly across back of sts; rep from * until 1 picked-up st rems.

To finish, k1, ssk, pass right st over left and off needle. Pull cut end through last st to secure.

Weave in loose ends. Lightly steam seams from WS and finger-press to reduce any bulk.

Insert folded edge of right front through buckle and pull buckle back far enough to reveal crocheted edge. Pin crocheted edge to left front waistband about 2" (5 cm) from side seam, curving the seam to follow the shape of the buckle. Whipstitch into place.

Steam the seam to set sts. Slide buckle into place to hide seam and secure folded edge into place.

Know Your Yarn: Bamboo

Bamboo fiber has a natural sheen and soft drape. The microscopic gaps in its structure allow it to breathe and regulate heat. It's therefore a comfortable choice for hot, humid weather. It is also highly absorbent, efficiently wicking away moisture from the body. Bamboo fiber accepts dye readily for splendid color clarity. It produces durable clothing that is easy to care for and shrinks only minimally in warm temperatures during washing and drying.

Bamboo, botanically classified as a grass, is one of the fastest growing renewable resources today. Crush the leaves and the inner pith of the bamboo stalk, send the mixture through a series of chemical processes, force the viscose bamboo through spinneret nozzles, then reconvert it to cellulose bamboo fiber thread, and spin it into yarn. Knit. Wear. Enjoy.

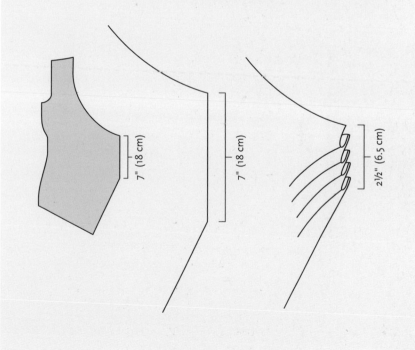

ZIGZAG SHELL

FINISHED SIZE
About 33 (35½, 37½, 39, 41, 43½, 45)"
(84 [90, 95, 99, 104, 110.5, 114.5] cm)
bust circumference.
Shell shown measures 35½" (90 cm).

YARN
DK weight (#3 Light).

Shown here: South West Trading Company
Terra (50% bamboo, 50% cotton; 120 yd
[110 m]/50 g): #434 blue (MC), 5 (6, 6, 6, 7,
7, 8) balls; #442 green (A), 3 (3, 3, 4, 4, 4,
4) balls, #422 purple (B), 1 ball.

NEEDLES
Body: size U.S. 5 (3.75 mm): 24" (60 cm)
circular (cir).
Edging: size U.S. 4 (3.5 mm): 16" (60 cm)
cir and 2 double-pointed (dpn).
*Adjust needle size if necessary to obtain the
correct gauge.*

NOTIONS
Waste yarn for holding sts; open-ring
markers (m); tapestry needle.

GAUGE
22 sts and 30 rows = 4" (10 cm) in St st on
larger needle.

Bold graphic blocks of color meet at an I-cord
zigzag for a dramatic shout of style in this
updated tee that features a straight body and
rounded neck. Choose from short-sleeve or
sleeveless options and mix two of your favorite
colors with a bold pop of a third to coordinate
with your wardrobe. Consider subtle neutrals,
vivid brights, similar tones, or opposite values
(such as black and white). Each triad palette will
individualize your fashion statement. The matte
and shine of the bamboo-cotton-blend yarn used
here offers visual texture that makes the colors
vibrate.

Back

With smaller needle, CO 91 (97, 103, 107, 113, 119, 123) sts. Do not join for working in rnds.

Row 1: (WS) P1, *k1, p1 through back loop (tbl); rep from * to last 2 sts, k1, p1.

Row 2: (RS) K1, p1, *k1tbl, p1; rep from * to last st, k1.

Rep these 2 rows once more, then work Row 1 once again—5 rows total.

Change to larger needle and work even in St st until piece measures 14½ (15, 15½, 16, 16½, 16½, 16½)" (37 [38, 39.5, 40.5, 42, 42, 42] cm) from CO, ending with a WS row.

Shape Armholes

BO 3 sts at beg of next 2 (2, 2, 2, 2, 2, 4) rows, then BO 2 sts at beg of foll 2 (4, 6, 6, 8, 8, 6) rows—81 (83, 85, 89, 91, 97, 99) sts rem.

Dec 1 st each end of needle every RS row 2 (3, 3, 3, 3, 4, 5) times—77 (77, 79, 83, 85, 89, 89) sts rem.

Work even in St st until armholes measure 6½ (6½, 7½, 7½, 7½, 8, 8)" (16.5 [16.5, 19, 19, 19, 20.5, 20.5] cm), ending with a WS row.

Shape Neck and Shoulders

Mark center 21 (21, 21, 21, 21, 23, 23) sts.

With RS facing, knit to marked sts, join new yarn and BO 21 (21, 21, 21, 21, 23, 23) marked sts, knit to end—28 (28, 29, 31, 32, 33, 33) sts rem each side.

Work each side separately as foll.

LEFT SIDE
Purl 1 WS row.

Work short-rows (see Glossary) as foll:

Short-Row 1: With RS facing, BO 9 (9, 9, 10, 10, 11, 11) sts, k8 (8, 9, 10, 10, 10, 10), wrap next st, turn work so WS is facing, purl to end—19 (19, 20, 21, 22, 22, 22) sts rem.

Row 2: (RS) Knit, working wrap tog with wrapped st as you go.

Row 3: Purl.

Place sts onto waste-yarn holder.

RIGHT SIDE
With WS facing, BO 9 (9, 9, 10, 10, 11, 11) sts pwise, purl to end—19 (19, 20, 21, 22, 22, 22) sts rem.

Knit 1 row even.

Short-Row 1: With WS facing, p8 (8, 9, 10, 10, 10, 10), wrap next st, turn work so RS is facing, knit to end.

Row 2: (WS) Purl, working wrap tog with wrapped st as you go.

Place sts onto waste-yarn holder.

Front

NOTE: One half of the front is worked in MC and the other half is worked in A. Change colors using the intarsia method, bringing the new color up from under the old at each color change to prevent holes from forming.

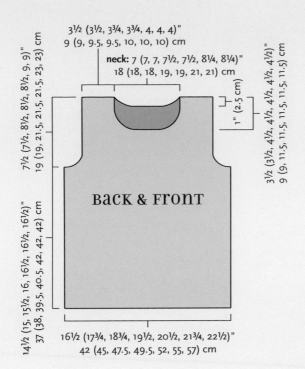

3½ (3½, 3¾, 3¾, 4, 4, 4)"
9 (9, 9.5, 9.5, 10, 10, 10) cm

neck: 7 (7, 7, 7½, 7½, 8¼, 8¼)"
18 (18, 18, 19, 19, 21, 21) cm

1" (2.5 cm)

7½ (7½, 8½, 8½, 8½, 9, 9)"
19 (19, 21.5, 21.5, 21.5, 23, 23) cm

3½ (3½, 4½, 4½, 4½, 4½, 4½)"
9 (9, 11.5, 11.5, 11.5, 11.5, 11.5) cm

back & front

14½ (15, 15½, 16, 16½, 16½, 16½)"
37 (38, 39.5, 40.5, 42, 42, 42) cm

16½ (17¾, 18¾, 19½, 20½, 21¾, 22½)"
42 (45, 47.5, 49.5, 52, 55, 57) cm

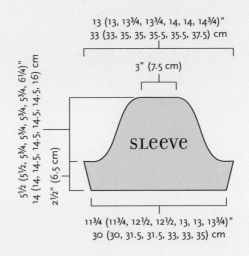

13 (13, 13¾, 13¾, 14, 14, 14¾)"
33 (33, 35, 35, 35.5, 35.5, 37.5) cm

3" (7.5 cm)

sleeve

5½ (5½, 5¾, 5¾, 5¾, 5¾, 6¼)"
14 (14, 14.5, 14.5, 14.5, 14.5, 16) cm

2½" (6.5 cm)

11¾ (11¾, 12½, 12½, 13, 13, 13¾)"
30 (30, 31.5, 31.5, 33, 33, 35) cm

With smaller needle and MC, CO 42 (45, 48, 50, 53, 56, 58) sts; with A CO 49 (52, 55, 57, 60, 63, 65) more sts onto same needle—91 (97, 103, 107, 113, 119, 123) sts total.

Mark the center st with open-ring marker to identify center st of chart and work in colors as established.

Row 1: (WS) P1, *k1, p1tbl; rep from * to last 2 sts, k1, p1.

Row 2: (RS): K1, p1, *k1tbl, p1; rep from * to last st, k1.

Rep these 2 rows once more, then work Row 1 once again—5 rows total.

Change to larger needle and St st, working Rows 6–104 (108, 112, 116, 120, 120, 120) of chart for color changes—piece measures about 14½ (15, 15½, 16, 16½, 16½, 16½)" (37 [38, 39.5, 40.5, 42, 42, 42] cm) from CO, ending with a WS row.

Shape Armholes

Cont working chart as established, BO 3 sts at beg of next 2 (2, 2, 2, 2, 2, 4) rows, then BO 2 sts at beg of foll 2 (4, 6, 6, 8, 8, 6) rows—81 (83, 85, 89, 91, 97, 99) sts rem.

Dec 1 st each end of needle every RS row 2 (3, 3, 3, 3, 4, 5) times—77 (77, 79, 83, 85, 89, 89) sts rem.

Cont through Row 134 (138, 142, 144, 150, 154, 154) of chart—armholes measure about 4 (4, 4, 4, 4, 4½, 4½)" (10 [10, 10, 10, 10, 11.5, 11.5] cm).

Shape Neck

Mark center 11 (11, 11, 13, 13, 15, 15) sts.

With RS facing, knit to marked sts, BO 11 (11, 11, 13, 13, 15, 15) marked sts, work to end—33 (33, 34, 35, 36, 37, 37) sts rem each side.

RIGHT SIDE
Purl 1 WS row.

At neck edge (beg of RS rows), BO 3 sts 2 times, then BO 2 sts 3 times—21 (21, 22, 23, 24, 25, 25) sts rem.

Dec row: (RS) K1, k2tog, knit to end—1 st dec'd.

Dec 1 st at neck edge in this manner every RS row 1 (1, 1, 1, 1, 2, 2) more time(s)—19 (19, 20, 21, 22, 22, 22) sts rem.

Work even until armhole measures 6½ (6½, 7½, 7½, 7½, 8, 8)" (16.5 [16.5, 19, 19, 19, 20.5, 20.5] cm), ending with a WS row.

Work short-rows as foll:

Short-Row 1: With RS facing, k9 (9, 10, 11, 11, 11, 11), wrap next st, turn work so WS is facing, purl to end.

Row 2: (RS) Knit, working wrap tog with wrapped st as you go.

Row 3: Purl.

Place sts onto waste-yarn holder.

With WS facing, join yarn to left front sts and at neck edge (beg of WS rows), BO 3 sts 2 times, then BO 2 sts 3 times—21 (21, 22, 23, 24, 25, 25) sts rem.

Dec row: (RS) Knit to last 3 sts, ssk, k1—1 st dec'd.

Dec 1 st at neck edge in this manner every RS row 1 (1, 1, 1, 1, 2, 2) more time(s)—19 (19, 20, 21, 22, 22, 22) sts rem.

Work even until armhole measures 6½ (6½, 7½, 7½, 7½, 8, 8)" (16.5 [16.5, 19, 19, 19, 20.5, 20.5] cm), ending with a RS row.

Work short-rows as foll:

Short-Row 1: With WS facing, p9 (9, 10, 11, 11, 11, 11), wrap next st, turn work so RS is facing, knit to end.

Row 2: (WS) Purl, working wrap tog with wrapped st as you go.

Place sts onto waste-yarn holder.

SLEEVES

NOTE: See page 63 for sleeveless option.

With smaller needle and MC for left sleeve or A for right sleeve, CO 65 (65, 69, 69, 71, 71, 75) sts. Do not join.

Row 1: (WS) P1, *k1, p1tbl; rep from * to last 2 sts, k1, p1.

Row 2: (RS) K1, p1, *k1tbl, p1; rep from * to last st, k1.

Rep these 2 rows once more, then work Row 1 once again—5 rows total.

Change to larger needle.

Inc row: (RS) K1, work left lifted inc (LLI; see Glossary) in next st, knit to last 2 sts, work right lifted inc (RLI; see Glossary) in next st, k1—2 sts inc'd.

Work 5 rows even.

Rep the last 6 rows once, then rep inc row once more—71 (71, 75, 75, 77, 77, 81) sts.

Work even until piece measures 2½" (6.5 cm) from CO, ending with a WS row.

ZIGZAG

MC   A   B

(chart rows labeled: 5, 10, 15, 20, 25, 30, 35, 40, 45, 50, 55, 60, 65, 70, 75, 80, 85, 90, 95, 100, 105, 110, 115, 120, 125, 130, 135, 140)

↑
center st

Shape Cap

BO 3 sts at beg of next 2 (2, 2, 2, 4, 4, 6) rows, then BO 2 sts at beg of foll 2 (2, 4, 4, 2, 2, 0) rows—61 (61, 61, 61, 61, 61, 63) sts rem.

Dec row: (RS) K1, k2tog, knit to last 3 sts, ssk, k1—2 sts dec'd.

Dec 1 st each end of needle in this manner every RS row 16 (16, 16, 16, 16, 16, 17) more times—27 sts rem.

BO 2 sts at beg of next 2 rows, then BO 3 sts at beg of foll 2 rows—17 sts rem.

BO all sts.

FINISHING

Using the steam method (see Glossary), block pieces to measurements, working from both sides. Allow to air-dry completely before moving.

Cont in rib as established until rib measures 1" (2.5 cm) from pick-up rnd.

BO all sts in patt.

Zigzag I-cord

With B and dpn, CO 3 sts.

Work 3-st I-cord (see Glossary) until piece measures about 35 (35, 35, 35, 35½, 35½, 35½)" (89 [89, 89, 89, 90, 90, 90] cm), slightly stretched.

Place sts on holder.

Pin cord along front zigzag from lower edge of rib to 3" (7.5 cm) below top of neck rib. With B threaded on a tapestry needle and working from WS, use whip-stitches (see Glossary) to secure I-cord to garment front, capturing just the back side of the I-cord when inserting tapestry needle from WS and adjusting fit as necessary. Add or subtract rows of I-cord as necessary to end at top of neck ribbing.

To finish, sl 1, k2tog, psso—1 st rem.

Cut yarn and pull tail through rem loop to secure.

Neck Border

With B and dpn, CO 3 sts.

Work 3-st I-cord until piece measures about 22" (56 cm) from CO, slightly stretched.

Place sts on holder.

Pin cord around neckline, covering neck rib pick-up and tucking beginning of I-cord just under the zigzag I-cord. With B threaded on a tapestry needle and working from WS, use backstitches (see Glossary) to secure I-cord around neckline, ending 3" (7.5 cm) before completing opening. Add or subtract rows of I-cord as necessary to end at beg of neckband. To finish, sl 1, k2tog, psso—1 st rem.

Cut yarn and pull tail through rem loop to secure. Secure rem 3" (7.5 cm) I-cord, tucking end under zigzag cord.

Seams

With matching yarn threaded on a tapestry needle, use the mattress st with ½ st seam allowance (see Glossary) to sew side and sleeve seams. Lightly steam-

Join Shoulders

Place 19 (19, 20, 21, 22, 22, 23) held right back sts onto one needle and 19 (19, 20, 21, 22, 22, 23) held right front sts onto a second needle. Hold needles parallel with RS of fabric facing tog. Use the three-needle method (see Glossary) to BO sts tog for right shoulder. Rep for left shoulder.

Neckband

With B, smaller, shorter cir needle, RS facing, and beg at right shoulder seam, pick up and knit 46 (46, 46, 48, 48, 50, 50) sts evenly spaced across back neck and 74 (74, 74, 76, 76, 80, 80) sts evenly spaced along front neck—120 (120, 120, 124, 124, 130, 130) sts total. Place marker (pm) and join for working in rnds.

Rnd 1: *K1, p1; rep from * around.

block seams. Steam I-cords from both RS and WS.

Pin sleeve cap into armhole, matching side and sleeve seams, matching center sleeve cap to shoulder seam and easing fullness at sleeve top. With crochet hook and working from the body (not the sleeve) side of the seam, use slip-st crochet (see Glossary) to join sleeve to body.

Lightly steam-block armhole seams.

sleeveless option

With MC or A to match front, smaller, shorter cir needle, RS facing, and beg at base of armhole, pick up and knit 82 (82, 94, 94, 94, 98, 98) sts evenly spaced around armhole. Pm and join for working in rnds.

Rnd 1: *K1, p1; rep from *.

Cont in rib as established until rib measures 1" (2.5 cm) from pick-up rnd.

BO all sts in patt.

tuscany lace

FINISHED SIZE
About 36 (40, 44, 48)" (91.5 [101.5, 112, 122] cm) bust circumference (see Notes).
Tunic shown measures 40" (101.5 cm).

YARN
DK weight (#3 Light).

Shown here: Classic Elite Firefly (75% viscose, 25% linen; 155 yd [146 m]/50 g): #7754 hyacinth (MC), 6 balls; #7777 Britannia (A), 2 (2, 3, 3) balls, and #7766 Sicily (B), 2 balls.

NEEDLES
Yoke: size U.S. 5 (3.75 mm): 24" (60 cm) circular (cir) plus an extra needle for three-needle bind-off.

Lace: sizes U.S. 8, 7, and 6 (5, 4.5, and 4 mm): 24" (60 cm) cir of each size.

Adjust needle size if necessary to obtain the correct gauge.

NOTIONS
Tapestry needle.

GAUGE
30 sts and 28 rows = 4" (10 cm) in Fair Isle patt on smallest needle.

19.5 sts and 26 rows = 4" (10 cm) in lace patt on size 6 (4 mm) needle, after blocking.

A simple Fair Isle rib stabilizes the yoke and cap sleeves while providing necessary structure for free flow of the lace pattern in this seemingly weightless tunic. The diamond-patterned lace literally and visually removes the weight, leaving a lovely drape of the rayon-linen yarn. A bit of skin is revealed through the open horizontal slit between the yoke and the lower tunic, offering visual balance between the two textures. This tunic is best featured over a solid color. Try it with a camisole and matching capris or a long tank dress—either way, you'll look great!

BACK YOKE

With B and smallest cir needle, CO 108 (116, 124, 132) sts. Do not join for working in rnds.

Set-up row: (RS) K1 with A (selvedge st), *k2 with A, k2 with B; rep from * to last 3 sts, k2 with A, k1 with A (selvedge st).

Row 1: (WS) P1A (selvedge st), *p2A, k2B; rep from * to last 3 sts, p2A, p1A (selvedge st).

Row 2: K1A (selvedge st), *k2A, p2B; rep from * to last 3 sts, k2A, k1A (selvedge st).

Rep the last 2 rows until piece measures 4½ (5, 5½, 5½)" (11.5 [12.5, 14, 14] cm) from CO, ending with a WS row.

Shape Neck

Keeping in patt, work 37 (41, 43, 47) sts, join a second ball of A and BO center 34 (34, 38, 38) sts knitwise, join a second ball of B and work to end—37 (41, 43, 47) sts rem each side.

Working each side separately, BO 10 (10, 12, 12) sts at each neck edge with A, working knitwise from RS and purlwise from WS—27 (31, 31, 35) sts rem each side.

Work even in patt until piece measures 5 (5½, 6, 6)" (12.5 [14, 15, 15] cm) from CO, ending with a WS row.

Place each set of sts onto waste-yarn holder, leaving 30" (76 cm) tail of each color for finishing.

FRONT YOKE

With A and smallest needle, CO 108 (116, 124, 132) sts. Do not join.

Set-up row: (RS) K1A (selvedge st), *k2A, k2B; rep from * to last 3 sts, k2A, k1A (selvedge st).

Next row: (WS) P1A (selvedge st), *p2A, k2B; rep from * to last 3 sts, p2A, p1A (selvedge st).

Work in short-rows (see Glossary) as foll:

....

NOTE: Do not work wraps tog with wrapped sts when you come to them.

....

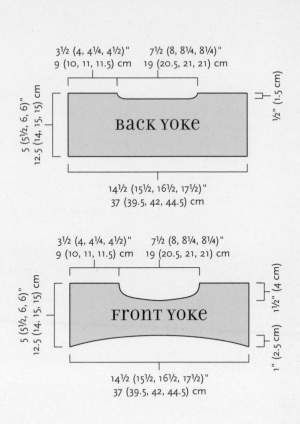

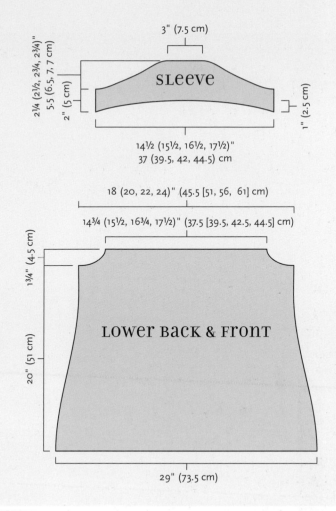

Short-Row 1: With RS facing, k3A, [p2B, k2A] 2 times, p1B, wrap next st, turn work so WS is facing, k1B, cross yarn by bringing A up from under B, [p2A, k2B] 2 times, p3A.

Short-Row 2: With RS facing, k3A, [p2B, k2A] 5 times, p1B, wrap next st, turn work so WS is facing, k1B, bring A up from under B, [p2A, k2B] 5 times, p3A.

Short-Row 3: With RS facing, k3A, [p2B, k2A] 8 times, p1B, wrap next st, turn work so WS is facing, k1B, bring A up from under B, [p2A, k2B] 8 times, p3A.

Short-Row 4: With RS facing, k3A, [p2B, k2A] 11 times, p1B, wrap next st, turn work so WS is facing, k1B, bring A up from under B, [p2A, k2B] 11 times, p3A.

Next row: (RS) K1A (selvedge st), *k2A, p2B; rep from * to last 3 sts, k2A, k1A (selvedge st).

Short-Row 5: With WS facing, p3A, [k2B, p2A] 2 times, k1B, wrap next st, turn work so RS is facing, p1B, bring A up from under B, [k2A, p2B] 2 times, k3A.

Short-Row 6: With WS facing, p3A, [k2B, p2A] 5 times, k1B, wrap next st, turn work so RS is facing, p1B, bring A up from under B, [k2A, p2B] 5 times, k3A.

Short-Row 7: With WS facing, p3A, [k2B, p2A] 8 times, k1B, wrap next st, turn work so RS is facing, p1B, bring A up from under B, [k2 A, p2 B] 8 times, k3A.

Short-Row 8: With WS facing, p3A, [k2B, p2A] 11 times, k1B, wrap next st, turn work so RS is facing, p1B, bring A up from under B, [k2A, p2B] 11 times, k3A.

Next row: P1A (selvedge st), *p2A, k2B; rep from * to last 3 sts, p2A, p1A (selvedge st).

Cont even in patt as established until piece measures 3½ (4, 4½, 4½)" (9 [10, 11.5, 11.5] cm) from CO at side edge, ending with a WS row.

Shape Neck

Keeping in patt, work 43 (47, 49, 53) sts, join a second ball of A and BO center 22 (22, 26, 26) sts knitwise, join second ball of B and work to end—43 (47, 49, 53) sts rem each side.

Working each side separately, with A and working knitwise from RS and purlwise from WS, at each neck edge BO 6 sts once, then BO 4 sts 2 times, then BO 2 sts 1 (1, 2, 2) time(s)—27 (31, 31, 35) sts rem.

Work even until piece measures 5 (5½, 6, 6)" (12.5 [14, 15, 15] cm) from CO, measured along side edge and ending with a WS row.

Place sts onto waste-yarn holder.

SLeeves

With A and smallest needle, CO 108 (116, 124, 124) sts. Do not join.

Work as for front yoke through all short-row shaping, then work even in Fair Isle as established until piece measures 2" (5 cm) from CO at side.

Shape Cap

Using A and carrying B along the WS and securing floats as needed, BO 9 sts at beg of next 2 rows, then BO 7 sts at beg of foll 2 rows, then BO 5 sts at beg of foll 2 rows, then BO 4 sts at beg of foll 6 (8, 10, 10) rows, then BO 5 sts at beg of foll 4 rows—22 sts rem.

BO all sts.

Lower Back

NOTE: Needle size changes while piece is in progress; read all the way through the foll section before proceeding.

With MC and size 8 (5 mm) needle, CO 114 sts. Do not join.

Purl 1 WS row. Work Rows 1–52 of Tuscany Lace chart 2 times, then work Rows 1–12 once again. *At the same*

Tuscany Lace

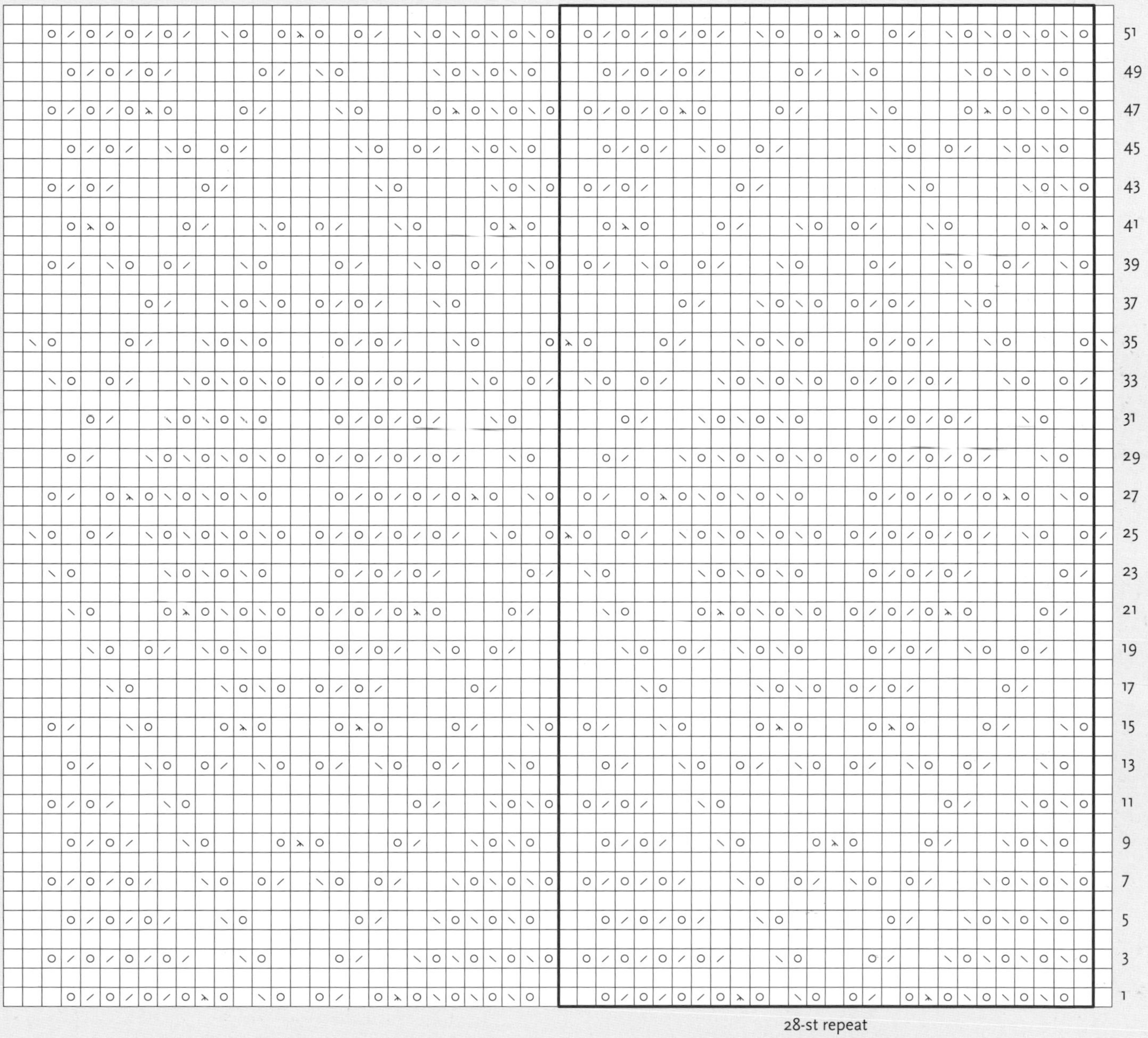

51
49
47
45
43
41
39
37
35
33
31
29
27
25
23
21
19
17
15
13
11
9
7
5
3
1

28-st repeat

| | k on RS; p on WS | | ○ | yo | | ╲ | ssk |
| | pattern repeat | | ╱ | k2tog | | ⅄ | sl 1, k2tog, psso |

time, when piece measures 8" (20.5 cm) from CO, change to size 7 (4.5 mm) needle, then, when piece measures 12" (30.5 cm) from CO, change to size 6 (4 mm) needle—piece measures about 17" (43 cm) from CO after chart has been worked for 64 rows, ending with Row 12 of chart.

Shape Armholes

NOTE: To make it easier to maintain the continuity of the lace pattern, place an open-ring marker after the first 14 sts and before the last 14 sts on the needle to denote the sts that will be eliminated during armhole shaping; remove the markers when the armhole shaping is complete.

Keeping in patt and beg with Row 13 of chart, BO 8 sts at beg of next 2 rows, then BO 2 sts at beg of foll 4 rows—90 sts rem.

Dec 1 st each end of needle every RS row 2 times—86 sts rem.

Work through Row 25 of chart.

Dec row: Purl, and *at the same time* work p2tog 14 (10, 4 , 0) times evenly spaced across row—72 (76, 82, 86) sts rem.

BO all sts kwise.

LOWER FRONT

CO and work the same as lower back.

FINISHING

Using the steam or wet-towel method (see Glossary), block Fair Isle pieces to measurements. Steam-block lace pieces. Allow to air dry thoroughly before moving.

Join Shoulders

Place each set of 27 (31, 31, 35) back yoke sts onto one smaller needle and corresponding front yoke sts onto another needle. Hold needles parallel with RS of fabric facing tog and, using the yarn tails, use the three-needle method (see Glossary) to BO the shoulder sts tog, matching colors as established.

Neckband

With A, smallest needle, and beg at right shoulder seam, pick up and knit 54 (54, 62, 62) sts evenly spaced across back neck and 70 (70, 74, 74) sts evenly spaced across front neck—124 (124, 136, 136) sts total.

Join for working in rnds. Purl 1 rnd. Change to MC and knit 1 rnd. BO all sts purlwise.

Seams

With MC threaded on a tapestry needle, use the mattress st with ½-st seam allowance (see Glossary) to sew side seams.

Use backstitches (see Glossary) to sew back lace panel to lower edge of back yoke, lapping yoke just slightly over BO edge of lace.

Pin front Fair Isle yoke to front lace panel for placement, lapping yoke just slightly over BO edge of lace for 4 (4, 4½, 5)" (10 [10, 11.5, 12.5] cm) in from each

armhole. Use backstitches to sew in place, leaving the center 6½ (7½, 7½, 7½)" (16.5 [19, 19, 19] cm) open for horizontal slit.

Sew side seams of sleeves using mattress st with 1 st seam allowance (see Glossary).

Armbands

With MC, smallest needle, and beg at center of underarm, pick up and knit 18 sts evenly spaced along lace portion of underarm, 32 (35, 38, 38) sts along yoke to shoulder seam, 32 (35, 38, 38) sts along yoke to lace section, then 18 sts to center of underarm—100 (106, 112, 112) sts total.

Join for working in rnds. Purl 1 rnd. BO all sts knitwise.

Pin sleeves into armholes, matching side to underarm seams, center sleeve cap to shoulder seam, and easing fullness of sleeve cap. With MC and crochet hook, and working from the body (not the sleeve) side of the garment, use slip-stitch crochet (see Glossary) to join sleeves to armholes.

Weave in loose ends. Steam seams to set sts.

paris LIGHTS

FINISHED SIZE
About 35 (37, 39, 41, 43, 45, 47, 49)" (89
[94, 99, 104, 109, 114.5, 119.5, 124.5] cm)
bust circumference, with 1½" (3.8 cm)
overlap.
Jacket shown measures 37" (94 cm).

YARN
DK weight (#3 Light).

Shown here: Plymouth Eros II (100%
nylon; 165 yd [155 m]/50 g): #4132 black/
gold, 6 (6, 7, 7, 8, 8, 9, 9) balls.

NEEDLES
Size U.S. 9 (4.5 mm): 24" (60 cm) circular
(cir) and extra needle the same size or
smaller for three-needle bind-off.

*Adjust needle size if necessary to obtain the
correct gauge.*

NOTIONS
Waste yarn for holding sts; size F/5
(4.5 mm) crochet hook; open-ring
markers (m); tapestry needle; one 1"
(2.5 cm) lightweight button or
decorative stick pin for closure.

GAUGE
16 sts and 24 rows = 4" (10 cm) in seed st.

Novelty yarn is at its best when it showcases
texture and color in a simple style. This elegant,
light jacket features a geometric stair-step
lower edge that dips in front and back and flares
gently from waist to hem and from elbow to cuff.
Worked in seed stitch, the sheen of this unique
ladder yarn captures the light and displays
remarkable color variation. The slim fit will
drape and mold to any figure—wear it open or
fastened with a single stick closure to define the
V-neck and enhance any dress style, especially
the basic little black one.

STITCH GUIDE

Seed Stitch Pattern *(even number of sts)*

Row 1: (RS) *K1, p1; rep from *.

Row 2: (WS) *P1, k1; rep from *.

Rep Rows 1 and 2 for patt.

NOTES

» Work seed stitch throughout entire garment, alternating knit and purl stitches; in subsequent rows, knit over purl stitches and purl over knit stitches.

» To ensure accuracy in measuring, spread knitting to its finished width before measuring for length. This may require transferring sts to waste yarn to spread to measurement.

BACK

CO 10 sts.

Work in seed st (see Stitch Guide) for 4 rows. With RS facing place an open-ring marker into front of work to indicate RS of garment.

Shape Lower Edge

*With RS facing, use the cable method (see Glossary) to CO 10 sts. Beg with the newly CO sts, work Row 1 of seed st to end of row.

With WS facing, use the cable method to CO 10 sts. Beg with the newly CO sts, work Row 2 of seed st to end of row.

Work even in seed st for 2 rows.

Rep from * once more—50 sts.

Cont in seed st, use the cable method to CO 8 (10, 12, 14, 10, 10, 10, 10) sts at beg of next 2 rows, then work 2 row even— 66 (70, 74, 78, 70, 70, 70, 70) sts.

Cont for your size as foll:

SIZES 43 (45, 47, 49)" ONLY

Cont in seed st, use the cable method to CO 6 (8, 10, 12) sts at beg of next 2 rows, then work 2 rows even—82 (86, 90, 94) sts.

ALL SIZES

Piece measures about 2½ (2½, 2½, 2½, 3¼, 3¼, 3¼, 3¼)" (6.5 [6.5, 6.5, 6.5, 8.5, 8.5, 8.5, 8.5] cm) from initial CO.

Cont even in seed st until piece measures 3½ (3½, 3½, 3½, 4, 4, 4, 4)" (9 [9, 9, 9, 10, 10, 10, 10] cm) from last CO, measured along side edge and ending with a WS row.

Dec Row 1: P2tog, *k1, p1; rep from * to last 2 sts, k2tog—2 sts dec'd.

Cont even in seed st until piece measures 5 (5, 5, 5, 5½, 5½, 6, 6)" (12.5 [12.5, 12.5, 12.5, 14, 14, 15, 15] cm) from

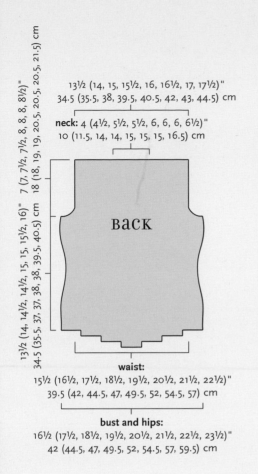

13½ (14, 15, 15½, 16, 16½, 17, 17½)"
34.5 (35.5, 38, 39.5, 40.5, 42, 43, 44.5) cm
neck: 4 (4½, 5½, 5½, 6, 6, 6, 6½)"
10 (11.5, 14, 14, 15, 15, 15, 16.5) cm
7 (7, 7½, 7½, 8, 8, 8, 8½)"
18 (18, 19, 19, 20.5, 20.5, 20.5, 21.5) cm
13½ (14, 14½, 14½, 15, 15, 15½, 16)"
34.5 (35.5, 37, 37, 38, 38, 39.5, 40.5) cm
BACK
waist:
15½ (16½, 17½, 18½, 19½, 20½, 21½, 22½)"
39.5 (42, 44.5, 47, 49.5, 52, 54.5, 57) cm
bust and hips:
16½ (17½, 18½, 19½, 20½, 21½, 22½, 23½)"
42 (44.5, 47, 49.5, 52, 54.5, 57, 59.5) cm
8½ (8¾, 9¼, 9½, 9¾, 10, 10¼, 10½)"
21.5 (22, 23.5, 24, 25, 25.5, 26, 26.5) cm
4¾ (4¾, 4¾, 5, 5, 5¼, 5½, 5½)"
12 (12, 12, 12.5, 12.5, 13.5, 14, 14) cm
7 (7, 7½, 7½, 8, 8, 8, 8½)"
18 (18, 19, 19, 20.5, 20.5, 20.5, 21.5) cm
13½ (14, 14½, 14½, 15, 15, 15½, 16)"
34.5 (35.5, 37, 37, 38, 38, 39.5, 40.5) cm
6 (6, 6½, 6½, 7, 7, 7, 7½)"
15 (15, 16.5, 16.5, 18, 18, 18, 19) cm
RIGHT FRONT
waist:
9½ (10, 10½, 11, 11½, 12, 12½, 13)"
24 (25.5, 26.5, 28, 29, 30.5, 31.5, 33) cm
bust and hips:
10 (10½, 11, 11½, 12, 12½, 13, 13½)"
25.5 (26.5, 28, 29, 30.5, 31.5, 33, 34.5) cm
13 (13, 13½, 14, 14½, 15, 15½, 16)"
33 (33, 34.5, 35.5, 37, 38, 39.5, 40.5) cm
4" (10 cm)
5 (5, 5½, 5½, 5¾, 6, 6, 6½)"
13 (13, 14, 14, 14.5, 15, 15, 16.5) cm
17 (17, 17½, 17½, 18, 18, 18, 18½)"
43 (43, 44.5, 44.5, 45.5, 45.5, 45.5, 47) cm
SLEEVE
middle: 11 (11, 11½, 12, 12½, 13, 13½, 14)"
28 (28, 29, 30.5, 31.5, 33, 34.5, 35.5) cm
lower edge: 12½ (12½, 13, 13½, 14, 14½, 15, 15½)"
31.5 (31.5, 33, 34.5, 35.5, 37, 38, 39.5) cm

last CO, measured along side edge and ending with a WS row.

Dec Row 2: K2tog, *p1, k1; rep from *to last 2 sts, p2tog—62 (66, 70, 74, 78, 82, 86, 90) sts rem.

Cont even in seed stitch until piece measures 9 (9, 9, 9, 9½, 9½, 10, 10)" (23 [23, 23, 23, 24, 24, 25.5, 25.5] cm) from last CO, measured along side edge and ending with a WS row.

Inc Row 1: K1f&b (see Glossary), p1, *k1, p1; rep from * to last 2 sts, k1f&b, k1—2 sts inc'd.

Cont even in seed st as established until piece measures 11 (11, 11, 11, 11½, 11½, 12, 12)" (28 [28, 28, 28, 29, 29, 30.5, 30.5] cm) from last CO, measured along side edge and ending with a WS row.

Inc Row 2: K1f&b, *k1, p1; rep from *to last 3 sts, k1, k1f&b, p1—66 (70, 74, 78, 82, 86, 90, 94) sts.

Cont even in seed st as established until piece measures 13½ (14, 14½, 14½, 15, 15, 15½, 16)" (34.5 [35.5, 37, 37, 38, 38, 39.5, 40.5] cm), measured along side edge.

Shape Armholes

Keeping in patt, BO 3 sts at beg of next 2 (2, 2, 2, 2, 2, 2, 4) rows, then BO 2 sts at beg of foll 2 (2, 2, 2, 2, 4, 4, 4) rows—56 (60, 64, 68, 72, 72, 76, 74) sts rem.

Dec 1 st each end of needle every RS row 1 (2, 2, 3, 4, 3, 4, 2) time(s)—54 (56, 60, 62, 64, 66, 68, 70) sts rem.

Cont even until armholes measure 7 (7, 7½, 7½, 8, 8, 8, 8½)" (18 [18, 19, 19, 20.5, 20.5, 20.5, 21.5] cm).

Place sts onto waste-yarn holder.

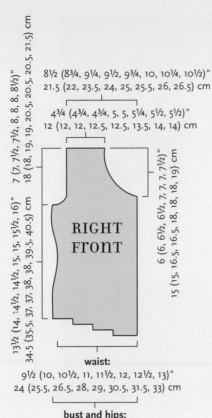

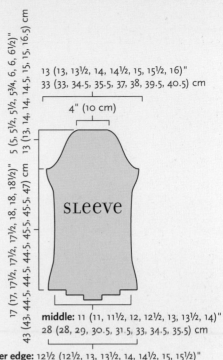

Rep from * once more—32 sts.

Cont in seed st, use the cable method to CO 8 (10, 12, 14, 10, 10, 10, 10) sts at beg of next row, then work 3 rows even—40 (42, 44, 46, 42, 42, 42, 42) sts.

Cont for your size as foll:

SIZES 43 (45, 47, 49)" ONLY
Cont in seed st, use the cable method to CO 6 (8, 10, 12) sts at beg of next row, then work 3 rows even —48 (50, 52, 54) sts.

ALL SIZES
Piece measures about 2½ (2½, 2½, 2½, 3¼ 3¼, 3¼, 3¼)" (6.5 [6.5, 6.5, 6.5, 8.5, 8.5, 8.5, 8.5] cm) from intiial CO.

Cont even in seed st until piece measures 3½ (3½, 3½, 3½, 4, 4, 4, 4)" (9 [9, 9, 9, 10, 10, 10, 10] cm) fom last CO, measured at side edge, ending with a WS row.

Dec row: Work in seed st to last 2 sts, k2tog or p2tog as necessary to maintain patt—1 st dec'd.

Cont even in seed st until piece measures 5 (5, 5, 5, 5½, 5½, 6, 6)" (12.5 [12.5, 12.5, 12.5, 14, 14, 15, 15] cm) from last CO, measured at side edge and ending with a WS row.

Rep dec row—38 (40, 42, 44, 46, 48, 50, 52) sts rem.

Cont even in seed st until piece measures 9 (9, 9, 9, 9½, 9½, 10, 10)" (23 [23, 23, 23, 24, 24, 25.5, 25.5] cm) from last CO, measured at side edge and ending with a WS row.

Inc row: Work in seed st to last 2 sts, k1f&b, k1 or p1 as necessary to maintain patt—1 st inc'd.

Cont even in seed st until piece measures 11 (11, 11, 11, 11½, 11½, 12, 12)" (28 [28, 28, 28, 29, 29, 30.5, 30.5] cm) from last CO, measured at side edge and ending with a WS row.

Rep inc row—40 (42, 44, 46, 48, 50, 52, 54) sts.

Cont even in seed st until piece measures 13½ (14, 14½, 14½, 15, 15, 15½, 16)" (34.5 [35.5, 37, 37, 38, 38, 39.5, 40.5] cm) from last CO, measured at side edge and ending with a RS row or optional RS buttonhole row (see below).

Optional buttonhole row: (RS) K1, p1, k1, yo, k2tog, work in seed st to end of row.

RIGHT Front

CO 12 sts.

Work in seed st for 4 rows. With RS facing, place an open-ring marker into front of work to indicate RS of garment.

Work 1 RS row even.

*With WS facing, use the cable method to CO 10 sts. Beg with the newly CO sts, *p1, k1; rep from * to end of row.

Work even in seed st for 3 rows.

Shape Armhole

NOTE: Neckline shaping is introduced while armhole shaping is in progress; read all the way through the following sections before proceeding.

At armhole edge (beg of WS rows), BO 3 sts 1 (1, 1, 1, 1, 1, 1, 2) time(s), then BO 2 sts 1 (1, 1, 1, 1, 2, 2, 2) times(s).

Dec 1 st each end of needle every RS row 1 (2, 2, 3, 4, 3, 4, 2) time(s)—6 (7, 7, 8, 9, 10, 11, 12) sts dec'd from armhole.

At the same time when 6 rows of armhole shaping have been worked, shape neck as foll.

Shape Neck

Cont armhole shaping as established, BO 2 sts at neck edge (beg of RS rows) 2 (2, 3, 3, 3, 3, 3, 3) times.

Dec 1 st at neck edge every RS row 11 (12, 12, 12, 13, 13, 13, 14) times—19 (19, 19, 20, 20, 21, 22, 22) sts rem after all armhole and neck shaping is complete.

Cont even until armhole measures 7 (7, 7½, 7½, 8, 8, 8, 8½)" (18 [18, 19, 19, 20.5, 20.5, 20.5, 21.5] cm).

Place sts onto waste-yarn holder.

Left Front

CO 12 sts.
Work in seed st for 4 rows. With RS facing, place an open-ring marker into front of work to indicate RS of garment.

*With RS facing, use the cable method to CO 10 sts. Beg with the newly CO sts, *k1, p1; rep from * to end of row.

Work even in seed st for 3 rows.

Rep from * once more—32 sts.

Cont in seed st, use the cable method to CO 8 (10, 12, 14, 10, 10, 10, 10) sts at beg of next row, then work 3 rows even—40 (42, 44, 46, 42, 42, 42, 42) sts.

Cont for your size as foll:

Know Your Yarn: Ladder Ribbon

Ladder ribbon yarn is made up of shimmering squares of color (usually some type of rayon or Tencel) suspended at regular intervals between two parallel black threads or very fine yarn. When knitted on large needles, this novelty yarn can produce a very lacy drape and elegant look.

SIZES 43 (45, 47, 49)" ONLY
Cont in seed st, use the cable method to CO 6 (8, 10, 12) sts at beg of next row, then work 3 rows even—48 (50, 52, 54) sts.

ALL SIZES
Piece measures about 2½ (2½, 2½, 2½, 3¼, 3¼, 3¼, 3¼)" (6.5 [6.5, 6.5, 6.5, 8.5, 8.5, 8.5, 8.5] cm) from initial CO.

Cont even in seed st until piece measures 3½ (3½, 3½, 3½, 4, 4, 4, 4)" (9 [9, 9, 9, 10, 10, 10, 10] cm) fom last CO, measured at side edge and ending with a WS row.

Dec row: K2tog or p2tog as necessary to maintain patt, work in seed st as established to end of row—1 st dec'd.

Cont even in seed st until piece measures 5 (5, 5, 5, 5½, 5½, 6, 6)" (12.5 [12.5, 12.5, 12.5, 14, 14, 15, 15] cm) from last CO, measured at side edge and ending with a WS row.

Rep dec row—38 (40, 42, 44, 46, 48, 50, 52) sts rem.

Cont even in seed st until piece measures 9 (9, 9, 9, 9½, 9½, 10, 10)" (23 [23, 23, 23, 24, 24, 25.5, 25.5] cm) from last CO, measured at side edge and ending with a WS row.

Inc row: K1f&b or p1f&b (see Glossary) as necessary to maintain patt, work in seed st as established to end of row—1 st inc'd.

Cont even in seed st until piece measures 11 (11, 11, 11, 11½, 11½, 12, 12)" (28 [28, 28, 28, 29, 29, 30.5, 30.5] cm) from last CO, measured at side edge and ending with a WS row.

Rep inc row—40 (42, 44, 46, 48, 50, 52, 54) sts.

Cont even in seed st until piece measures 13½ (14, 14½, 14½, 15, 15, 15½, 16)" (34.5 [35.5, 37, 37, 38, 38, 39.5, 40.5] cm) from last CO, measured at side edge and ending with a WS row.

Shape Armhole

NOTE: Neckline shaping is introduced while armhole shaping is in progress; read all the way through the following sections before proceeding.

At armhole edge (beg of RS rows) BO 3 sts 1 (1, 1, 1, 1, 1, 1, 2) time(s), then BO 2 sts 1 (1, 1, 1, 1, 2, 2, 2) times(s).

Dec 1 st each end of needle every RS row 1 (2, 2, 3, 4, 3, 4, 2) time(s)—6 (7, 7, 8, 9, 10, 11, 12) sts dec'd from armhole.

At the same time, when 6 rows of armhole shaping have been worked, shape neck as foll.

Shape Neck

Cont armhole shaping as established, BO 2 sts at neck edge (beg of WS rows) 2 (2, 3, 3, 3, 3, 3, 3) times.

Dec 1 st at neck edge every RS row 11 (12, 12, 12, 13, 13, 13, 14) times—19 (19, 19, 20, 20, 21, 22, 22) sts rem after all armhole and neck shaping is complete.

Cont even until armhole measures 7 (7, 7½, 7½, 8, 8, 8, 8½)" (18 [18, 19, 19, 20.5, 20.5, 20.5, 21.5] cm).

Place sts onto waste-yarn holder.

SLEEVES

CO 10 sts.

Work in seed st for 4 rows. With RS facing, place an open-ring marker into front of work to indicate RS of garment.

Shape Lower Edge

Next row: (RS) Use the cable method to CO 10 (10, 10, 11, 11, 12, 12, 13) sts, then beg with the newly CO sts, work in seed st as established to end of row.

Next row: (WS) CO 10 (10, 10, 11, 11, 12, 12, 13) sts as before, then beg with newly CO sts, work in seed st as

established to end of row—30 (30, 30, 32, 32, 34, 34, 36) sts.

Work 2 rows even in seed st.

Next row: (RS) CO 10 (10, 11, 11, 12, 12, 13, 13) sts as before, then work in seed st as established to end of row.

Next row: (WS) CO 10 (10, 11, 11, 12, 12, 13, 13) sts as before, then work in seed st as established to end of row—50 (50, 52, 54, 56, 58, 60, 62) sts.

Work 8 rows even in patt.

Dec row: (RS) K2tog or p2tog as necessary to maintain patt, work in seed st as established to the last 2 sts, k2tog or p2tog as necessary to maintain patt—2 sts dec'd.

Work 7 rows even in seed st.

Rep the last 8 rows 2 more times—44 (44, 46, 48, 50, 52, 54, 56) sts rem.

Work even in seed st until piece measures 13½" (34.5 cm) from CO, ending with a WS row.

Inc row: (RS) K1f&b, work in patt to last 2 sts, k1f&b, k1—2 sts inc'd.

Work 7 rows even in patt.

Rep the last 8 rows 3 more times—52 (52, 54, 56, 58, 60, 62, 64) sts.

Work even until piece measures 17 (17, 17½, 17½, 17½, 18, 18, 18½)" (43 [43, 44.5, 44.5, 44.5, 45.5, 45.5, 47] cm) from last CO at sleeve seam edge, ending with a WS row.

Shape Cap

BO 3 sts at beg of next 2 rows, then BO 2 sts at beg of foll 2 (2, 2, 4, 4, 4, 6, 6) rows—42 (42, 44, 42, 44, 46, 44, 46) sts rem.

Dec 1 st each end of needle every RS row 13 (13, 14, 13, 14, 15, 14, 15) times—16 sts rem.

BO all sts.

FINISHING

Using the wet-towel method (see Glossary), block pieces to measurements.

Join Shoulders

Return 54 (56, 60, 62, 64, 66, 68, 70) held back sts onto one needle and 19 (19, 19, 20, 20, 21, 22, 22) held right front sts onto another needle. With RS facing tog, use the three-needle method (see Glossary) to BO right front and back sts tog for right shoulder. BO the next 16 (18, 22, 22, 24, 24, 24, 26) back sts singly. Place 19 (19, 19, 20, 20, 21, 22, 22) held left front sts onto second needle and, with RS facing tog, use the three-needle method to BO left front and rem back sts tog for left shoulder.

Seams

With yarn threaded on a tapestry needle, use a mattress st for seed stitch (see Glossary) to sew side and sleeve seams.

Pin sleeve cap into armhole, matching side and sleeve seams, matching center sleeve cap with shoulder seam, and easing in fullness at top of cap as necessary. With a crochet hook and working from the body (not the sleeve) side of the join, use slip st crochet method (see Glossary) to join cap into armhole.

Weave in loose ends. Lightly steam-block seams and finger-press to reduce bulk, being careful not to touch iron to knitted fabric (which might cause it to melt).

Sew button to left front opposite optional buttonhole, if desired.

KATHMANDU

FINISHED SIZE
About 33 (35, 37, 39, 41, 43, 45)" (84 [89, 94, 99, 109, 114.5] cm) bust circumference. Shell shown measures 35" (89 cm).

YARN
Sportweight (#2 Light).

Shown here: South West Trading Company Oasis (100% soysilk; 240 yd [219 m]/100 g): #063 red (MC), 5 (6, 6, 6, 7, 7, 7) balls; #065 sapphire (CC) 1 ball.

NEEDLES
Size U.S. 6 (4 mm): 24" (60 cm) circular (cir).

Adjust needle size if necessary to obtain the correct gauge.

NOTIONS
Waste yarn for holding sts; markers and open-ring marker (m); size E/5 (3.5 mm) crochet hook; tapestry needle; sharp-point sewing needle; contrasting thread.

GAUGE
23 sts and 30 rows = 4" (10 cm) in St st.

Inspired by the ethnic flavor of India's flamboyantly colorful clothing, rich vibrant colors and embroidery find their way into this sleeveless top. The bodice features princess shaping lines that are defined by raised slipped stitches. The gently flared peplum ends in undulating folds, thanks to a fluid bamboo tape yarn. Chain-stitch crochet and embroidery embellishments (French knots, daisy, and fly stitches) highlight the low U-neckline shape and strengthen the artistry of the design. Be as bold as the color and try this top over leggings and heels for top-shelf class!

Work 3 rows even.

Dec Row 2: K1, slip marker (sl m), *knit to 2 sts before next m, k2tog, sl m; rep from * 9 more times, k1—10 sts dec'd.

Work 3 rows even.

Rep the last 4 rows 11 more times—102 (112, 112, 122, 122, 132, 142) sts rem.

Next row: K1 (selvedge st), sl m, [knit to m, remove m] 1 (0, 2, 0, 3, 1, 0) time(s), [knit to 2 sts before next m, k2tog, sl m] 8 (10, 6, 10, 4, 8, 10) times, [knit to m, remove m] 1 (0, 2, 0, 3, 1, 0) time(s)—94 (102, 106, 112, 118, 124, 132) sts rem; piece measures about 7½" (19 cm) from CO.

With WS facing, BO all sts purlwise, working the first 2 sts and the last 2 sts as p2tog for sizes 35 and 45 only—94 (100, 106, 112, 118, 124, 130) sts rem.

Do not cut yarn. Enlarge last loop and insert ball through the loop to secure.

Bodice

With RS facing and yarn already attached, pick up and knit 1 st in back loop of each BO st—94 (100, 106, 112, 118, 124, 130) sts.

Purl 1 (WS) row.

Row 1: (RS) K26 (28, 30, 32, 34, 36, 38), sl 1 pwise, k40 (42, 44, 46, 48, 50, 52), sl 1 kwise, k26 (28, 30, 32, 34, 36, 38).

Row 2: Purl.

Rep these 2 rows until piece measures 7 (7, 6¾, 6½, 6½, 6, 6)" (18 [18, 17, 16.5, 16.5, 15, 15] cm) from pick-up row.

Princess Shaping

NOTE: Armhole shaping is introduced while princess shaping is in progress; read all the way through the following sections before proceeding.

Row 1: (RS) Knit to 2 sts before slipped st, sl 1, k1, psso, sl 1 pwise, M1L (see Glossary), knit to next slipped st, M1R (see Glossary), sl 1 kwise, k2tog, knit to end—no change to stitch count.

BACK

With MC, CO 232 (242, 242, 252, 252, 262, 272) sts. Do not join for working in rnds.

Beg and end with a WS row, work in St st (knit RS rows; purl WS rows) for 3 rows.

Dec Row 1: K1 (selvedge st), place marker (pm), *k21 (22, 22, 23, 23, 24, 25), k2tog, pm; rep from * 9 more times, k1 (selvedge st)—222 (232, 232, 242, 242, 252, 262) sts rem.

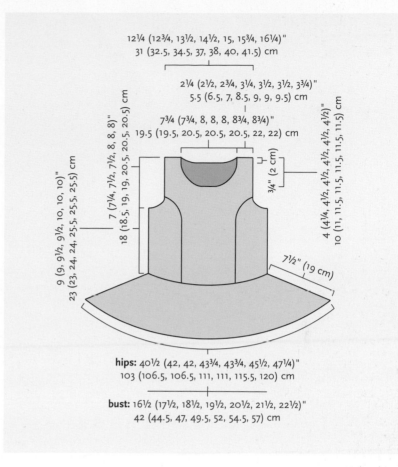

12¼ (12¾, 13½, 14½, 15, 15¾, 16¼)"
31 (32.5, 34.5, 37, 38, 40, 41.5) cm

2¼ (2½, 2¾, 3¼, 3½, 3½, 3¾)"
5.5 (6.5, 7, 8.5, 9, 9, 9.5) cm

7¾ (7¾, 8, 8, 8, 8¾, 8¾)"
19.5 (19.5, 20.5, 20.5, 20.5, 22, 22) cm

7 (7¼, 7½, 7½, 8, 8, 8)"
18 (18.5, 19, 19, 20.5, 20.5, 20.5) cm

¾" (2 cm)

4 (4¼, 4½, 4½, 4½, 4½, 4½)"
10 (11, 11.5, 11.5, 11.5, 11.5, 11.5) cm

9 (9, 9½, 10, 10, 10, 10)"
23 (23, 24, 24, 25.5, 25.5, 25.5) cm

7½" (19 cm)

hips: 40½ (42, 42, 43¾, 43¾, 45½, 47¼)"
103 (106.5, 106.5, 111, 111, 115.5, 120) cm

bust: 16½ (17½, 18½, 19½, 20½, 21½, 22½)"
42 (44.5, 47, 49.5, 52, 54.5, 57) cm

Row 2: Purl.

Rep last 2 rows 12 (13, 14, 15, 16, 17, 18) more times.

Shape Armholes

At the same time when piece measures 9 (9, 9½, 9½, 10, 10, 10)" (23 [23, 24, 24, 25.5, 25.5, 25.5] cm) from pick-up row, ending with a WS row, BO 4 (5, 5, 5, 5, 5, 5) sts at beg of next 2 rows, then BO 3 (4, 4, 4, 4, 4, 4) sts at beg of next 2 rows, then BO 3 (2, 2, 2, 3, 3, 3) sts at beg of foll 2 (2, 2, 4, 2, 2, 2) rows, then BO 0 (0, 0, 0, 2, 2, 2) sts at beg of next 0 (0, 0, 0, 2, 2, 4) rows—20 (22, 22, 26, 28, 28, 32) sts BO.

Dec row: (RS) K1, k2tog, knit to last 3 sts, ssk, k1—2 sts dec'd.

Dec 1 st each end of needle in this manner every RS row 1 (1, 2, 1, 1, 2, 1) more time(s)—70 (74, 78, 82, 86, 90, 94) sts rem.

Work even until armholes measure 6¼ (6½, 6¾, 6¾, 7¼, 7¼, 7¼)" (16 (16.5, 17, 17, 18.5, 18.5, 18.5] cm), ending with a WS row.

Shape Neck

Mark center 20 (20, 22, 22, 22, 22, 22) sts.

With RS facing, knit to m, join new yarn and BO center 20 (20, 22, 22, 22, 22, 22) sts, knit to end—25 (27, 28, 30, 32, 34, 36) sts rem each side.

Working each side separately, BO 8 (8, 8, 8, 8, 9, 9) sts at each neck edge once, then BO 4 (4, 4, 4, 4, 5, 5) sts once—13 (15, 16, 18, 20, 20, 22) sts rem each side.

Work even until armholes measure 7 (7¼, 7½, 7½, 8, 8, 8)" (18 [18.5, 19, 19, 20.5, 20.5, 20.5] cm), ending with a WS row.

Place sts onto waste-yarn holder.

With RS facing, knit to m, join new yarn and BO center 12 (12, 12, 12, 12, 14, 14) sts, knit to end—29 (31, 33, 35, 37, 38, 40) sts rem each side.

Working each side separately, BO 5 (5, 5, 5, 5, 6, 6) sts at each neck edge once, then BO 3 sts 1 (1, 2, 2, 2, 2, 2) time(s), then BO 2 sts 2 (2, 1, 1, 1, 1, 1) time(s)—17 (19, 20, 22, 24, 24, 26) sts rem each side.

Dec row: (RS) For right shoulder, k1, k2tog, knit to end; for left shoulder, knit to last 3 sts, ssk, k1—1 st dec'd each side.

Work 3 rows even.

Rep the last 4 rows 3 more times—13 (15, 16, 18, 20, 20, 22) sts rem each side.

Work even until armholes measure 7 (7¼, 7½, 7½, 8, 8, 8)" (18 [18.5, 19, 19, 20.5, 20.5, 20.5] cm), ending with a WS row.

Place sts onto waste-yarn holder.

Front

CO and work same as back until armholes measure 3 (3, 3, 3, 3½, 3½, 3½)" (7.5 [7.5, 7.5, 7.5, 9, 9, 9] cm) and piece measures about 12 (12, 12½, 1½, 13½, 13½, 13½)" (30.5 [30.5, 31.5, 31.5, 34.5, 34.5, 34.5] cm) from peplum pick-up row.

Shape Neck

Mark center 12 (12, 12, 12, 12, 14, 14) sts.

FINISHING

Using the steam method (see Glossary), block to measurements. Allow to air-dry thoroughly before moving.

Seams

Place 13 (15, 16, 18, 20, 20, 22) held right back sts onto one needle and 13 (15, 16, 18, 20, 20, 22) held right front sts onto another needle. Hold needles parallel with RS of fabric facing tog. Use the three-needle method (see Glossary) to BO sts tog for right shoulder. Rep for left shoulder.

With yarn threaded on a tapestry needle, use the mattress st with ½ st seam allowance (see Glossary) to sew side seams, being careful to match top of peplum on front and back.

Armbands

With smaller cir needle, RS facing, and beg at underarm seam, pick up and knit 45 (46, 47, 47, 49, 49) sts evenly spaced to shoulder seam and 45 (46, 47, 47, 49, 49) sts to center of underarm—90 (92, 94, 94, 98, 98) sts total.

Pm and join for working in rnds. Purl 1 rnd, then knit 1 rnd.

BO all sts purlwise.

Neckband

With smaller cir needle, RS facing, and beg at right shoulder seam, pick up and knit 59 (59, 61, 61, 61, 63, 63) sts evenly spaced across back neck and 68 (68, 70, 70, 70, 74, 74) sts evenly spaced along front neck—127 (127, 131, 131, 131, 137, 137) sts total.

Pm and join for working in rnds. Purl 1 rnd, then knit 1 rnd.

BO all sts pwise.

Embroidery

With contrasting thread, work running sts (see Glossary) to mark placement for embroidery about ¾" (2 cm) from neck edge on front and back and making a U-shape about 2" (5 cm) long and 1¼" (3.2 cm) wide at center front.

With CC, crochet hook, and beg at right shoulder seam, work crochet chain stitch (see Glossary) along running stitch guide. To finish, work last chain st 1 st away from first st worked, cut yarn, and pull cut end through last loop.

Thread tail on needle and insert needle behind the first chain st, staying on RS of work, then back to WS at same point where the cut end emerged from the last chain st.

With CC threaded on a tapestry needle, work daisy sts with French knots, fly stitch, and French knots as shown in photos.

Lightly steam to set sts.

oriGami FLOWer

FINISHED SIZE
About 32 (34, 36, 38, 40, 42, 44, 46)" (81.5 [86.5, 91.5, 96.5, 101.5, 106.5, 112, 117] cm) bust circumference.
Shell shown measures 34" (86.5 cm).

YARN
Light weight (#2 Fine).
Shown here: Classic Elite Allegoro (70% organic cotton, 30% linen; 152 yd [139 m]/50 g): #5685 orange zest (MC) 4 (5, 5, 5, 6, 6, 6, 7) balls; #5656 larkspur (A) and #5616 parchment (B), 1 (1, 2, 2, 2, 2, 2, 2) ball(s) each.

NEEDLES
Body: size U.S. 5 (3.75 mm): 24" (60 cm) circular (cir).

Edging: size U.S. 4 (3.5 mm): 16" (40 cm) cir.

Adjust needle size if necessary to obtain the correct gauge.

NOTIONS
Waste yarn for holding sts; open-ring marker; size E/4 (3.5 mm) crochet hook; tapestry needle.

GAUGE
22 sts and 28 rows = 4" (10 cm) in St st on larger needle.

Flattering diagonals sweep across the front of this whimsical, yet elegant, V-neck shell to separate stripes from solids. Sleeveless and slightly shaped at the waist, a harmonious triadic color arrangement defines each section of construction. For this version, colors are similar in value for a soft look—feel free to get bold with your own combinations. The curiously inventive three-dimensional folded flower is optional; knit a plain band for a sportier look. The comfort of cotton and the classic texture of linen are blended in this yarn, giving you the best of both fibers.

BACK

With MC and larger needle, CO 99 (105, 111, 117, 121, 127, 133, 139) sts. Do not join for working in rnds.

Set-up row: (WS) Purl.

Row 1: (RS) *K1, p1; rep from * to last st, k1.

Row 2: Purl.

Rep the last 2 rows once more.

Work even in St st until piece measures 3" (7.5 cm) from CO, ending with a WS row.

Dec row: (RS) K2, k2tog, knit to last 4 sts, ssk, k2—2 sts dec'd.

Work 5 rows even. Rep the last 6 rows 8 more times—81 (87, 93, 99, 103, 109, 115, 121) sts rem.

Work even until piece measures 13" (33 cm) from CO, ending with a WS row.

Inc row: (RS) K2, work left lifted inc (LLI; see Glossary) in next st, knit to last 3 sts, work right lifted inc (RLI; see Glossary) in next st, k2—2 sts inc'd.

Work 7 rows even. Rep the last 8 rows once, then rep inc row once more—87 (93, 99, 105, 109, 115, 121, 127) sts.

Work even until piece measures 16" (40.5 cm) from CO, ending with a WS row.

Shape Armholes

BO 3 (3, 4, 5, 4, 5, 5, 5) sts at beg of next 2 rows, then BO 2 (2, 2, 2, 3, 3, 3, 3) sts at beg of foll 2 (2, 4, 4, 2, 2, 2, 2) rows, then BO 0 (0, 0, 0, 2, 2, 2, 2) sts at beg of foll 0 (0, 0, 0, 4, 4, 4, 6) rows—77 (83, 83, 87, 87, 91, 97, 99) sts rem.

Dec row: (RS) K2, k2tog, knit to last 4 sts, ssk, k2—2 sts dec'd.

Dec 1 st each end of needle in this manner every RS row 0 (2, 1, 1, 1, 2, 3, 3) more time(s)—75 (77, 79, 83, 83, 85, 89, 91) sts rem.

Work even until armholes measure 7 (7, 7, 7½, 7½, 7½, 8, 8)" (18 [18, 18, 19, 19, 19, 20.5, 20.5] cm), ending with a WS row.

Place sts onto waste-yarn holder.

LOWER FRONT

With MC, CO and work as for back until a total of 5 (5, 5, 4, 4, 4, 4, 4) decs have been worked at each side edge and 1 (1, 1, 5, 5, 5, 5, 5) row(s) even has been worked after the last dec row—89 (95, 101, 109, 113, 119, 125, 131) sts rem.

Right Front

NOTE: Right front curve and neck shaping and armhole shaping are introduced while side shaping is in progress; read all the way through the following sections before proceeding.

Cont shaping right side edge (end of RS rows) as established, and *at the same time* shape front curve at beg of RS rows as foll: BO 5 (5, 8, 8, 5, 7, 5, 7) sts 2 (5, 1, 1, 6, 1, 8, 1) time(s), then BO 4 (0, 5, 4, 4, 5, 0, 5) sts 3 (0, 4, 6, 1, 6, 0, 7) time(s), then BO 3 sts 3 times, then BO 2 sts 5 times—41 (44, 47, 51, 53, 56, 59, 61) sts BO.

Dec row: (RS) K1, k2tog, knit to end.

Dec 1 st in this manner at beg of every RS row 23 more times.

[Rep dec row, then work 3 rows even] 10 times—34 sts dec'd total.

Also at the same time, when piece measures 16" (40.5 cm) from CO, shape armhole as foll.

SHAPE ARMHOLE

At armhole edge (beg of WS rows) BO 3 (3, 4, 5, 4, 5, 5, 5) sts once, then BO 2 (2, 2, 2, 3, 3, 3, 3) sts 1 (1, 2, 2, 1, 1, 1, 1) time(s), then BO 0 (0, 0, 0 2, 2, 2, 2) sts 0 (0, 0, 0, 2, 2, 2, 3) times—5 (5 , 8, 9, 11, 12, 12, 14) sts dec'd.

Dec row: (RS) Knit to last 4 sts, k2tog, k2—1 st dec'd.

Dec 1 st at armhole edge in this manner every RS row 0 (2, 1, 1, 1, 2, 3, 3) more time(s)—7 (8, 9, 11, 11, 12, 14, 16) sts rem when all front, armhole, and neck shaping is complete.

Work even until armholes measure 7 (7, 7, 7½, 7½, 7½, 8, 8)" (18 [18, 18, 19, 19, 19, 20.5, 20.5] cm), ending with a WS row.

Place sts onto waste-yarn holder.

Left Front

NOTES: Left front curve, neck, side, and armhole shaping are each introduced in progression; read all the way through the following sections before proceeding.

A and B alternate every 2 rows; pick up the desired color at beg of every RS row, carrying the unworked yarn loosely along left side edge.

With B (A, B, A, A, B, B, B) and larger needle, CO 5 (4, 4, 3, 5, 3, 6, 9) sts. Do not join.

Purl 1 WS row, then knit 1 RS row.

Next row: (WS) Use the knitted method (see Glossary) to CO 4 sts, purl CO sts, purl to end.

Next row: Change color and knit 1 row.

Next row: Use the knitted method to CO 4 sts, purl CO sts, purl to end.

Rep the last 2 rows 0 (1, 2, 3, 3, 4, 4, 4) more time(s)—8 (12, 16, 20, 20. 24, 24, 24) sts CO.

Cont to alternate colors every 2 rows, shape front curve as foll: Use the knitted method to CO 3 sts at beg of next 3 WS rows, then CO 2 sts at beg of foll 5 WS row—32 (35, 39, 42, 44, 46, 49, 52) sts total CO on front edge (including initial CO).

Inc row: (RS) Knit to last st, M1 (see Glossary), k1—1 st inc'd.

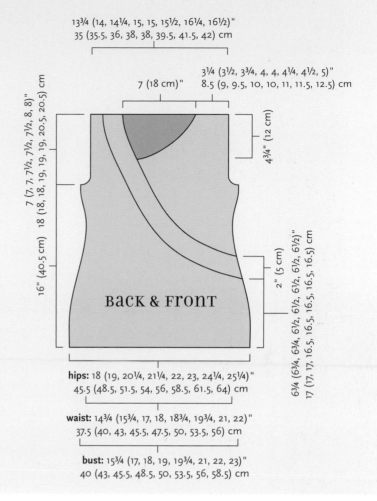

13¾ (14, 14¼, 15, 15, 15½, 16¼, 16½)"
35 (35.5, 36, 38, 38, 39.5, 41.5, 42) cm

3¼ (3½, 3¾, 4, 4, 4¼, 4½, 5)"
8.5 (9, 9.5, 10, 10, 11, 11.5, 12.5) cm

7 (18 cm)"

4¾ (12 cm)

7 (7, 7, 7½, 7½, 7½, 8, 8)"
18 (18, 18, 19, 19, 19, 20.5, 20.5) cm

16" (40.5 cm)

2" (5 cm)

6¾ (6¾, 6¾, 6½, 6½, 6½, 6½, 6½)"
17 (17, 17, 16.5, 16.5, 16.5, 16.5, 16.5) cm

BACK & FRONT

hips: 18 (19, 20¼, 21¼, 22, 23, 24¼, 25¼)"
45.5 (48.5, 51.5, 54, 56, 58.5, 61.5, 64) cm

waist: 14¾ (15¾, 17, 18, 18¾, 19¾, 21, 22)"
37.5 (40, 43, 45.5, 47.5, 50, 53.5, 56) cm

bust: 15¾ (17, 18, 19, 19¾, 21, 22, 23)"
40 (43, 45.5, 48.5, 50, 53.5, 56, 58.5) cm

Inc 1 st at end of every RS row in this manner 18 more times—19 sts inc'd total.

Then inc in this manner every 4 rows 4 times—4 sts inc'd.

At the same time beg on the 2nd (3rd, 1st, 2nd, 2nd, 3rd, 3rd, 3rd) color-change row, shape side as foll.

SHAPE SIDE

Dec row: (RS) K2, ssk, knit to end—1 st dec'd.

Rep dec row every 6 rows 1 (1, 2, 2, 2, 3, 3, 3) more time(s)—2 (2, 3, 3, 3, 4, 4, 4) sts dec'd total.

Cont working COs as established, work right side edge even until piece measures 4¾" (12 cm) from CO, ending with a WS row.

SHAPE NECK

Cont front shaping and color stripes as established and working purlwise, at neck edge (beg of WS row), BO 5 sts 2 times, then BO 4 sts once, then BO 3 sts once, then BO 2 sts 3 times—23 neck sts BO.

Dec row: (RS) Knit to last 3 sts, k2tog, k1—1 st dec'd.

Rep dec row every RS row 8 (8, 8, 8, 6, 6, 5) more times—18 (19, 20, 22, 22, 23, 25, 27) sts rem when all front curve and armhole shaping is complete.

Cont even until armhole measures 7 (7, 7, 7½, 7½, 7½, 8, 8)" (18 [18, 18, 19, 19, 19, 20.5, 20.5] cm), ending with a WS row.

Place sts onto waste-yarn holder.

FRONT BAND

With A and smaller needle, CO 11 sts. Do not join.

Short-Row 1: With WS facing, p5, wrap next st (see Glossary), turn work so RS is facing, k5.

Cont even in St st, hiding wrap when you come to it, until piece measures about about 22½ (23, 23, 23½, 23½, 23½, 24, 24)" (57 [58.5, 58.5, 59.5, 59.5, 59.5, 61, 61] cm) from CO, ending with a WS row. Do not cut yarn. Place sts on holder.

FINISHING

Use the steam or wet-towel method (see Glossary) to block pieces to measurements. Allow to air-dry thoroughly before moving.

Assembling

Lay front pieces on flat surface with front band between the center fronts, with left edge of band to right center front and right edge of band to left center front.

Use open-ring markers to mark both edges of the band at the beg of the left front V. Pin in place up to the markers.

With A, beg at side edge, and using a mattress st with ½ st seam allowance (see Glossary), sew left edge of band to right front to marked position.

Sew right edge of band to left front from side edge to beg of V-neck.

Inc row: (RS) K2, work left lifted inc (LLI; see Glossary) in next st, work to end—1 st inc'd.

Work 7 rows even. Rep the last 8 rows once, then rep inc row once more—3 sts inc'd total.

Work even on side edge in stripes as established until side edge measures 7¾" (19.5 cm) from CO, ending with a WS row.

SHAPE ARMHOLE

NOTE: Front curve shaping continues as armhole is shaped; read all the way through the following section before proceeding.

Cont shaping front curve as established, at armhole edge (beg of RS rows) BO 3 (3, 4, 5, 4, 5, 5, 5) sts once, then BO 2 (2, 2, 2, 3, 3, 3, 3) sts 1 (1, 2, 2, 1, 1, 1, 1) time(s), then BO 0 (0, 0, 0 2, 2, 2, 2) sts 0 (0, 0, 0, 2, 2, 2, 3) times—5 (5 , 8, 9, 11, 12, 12, 14) sts BO.

Dec row: (RS) K2, k2tog, knit to end—1 st dec'd.

Dec 1 st at armhole edge in this manner every RS row 0 (2, 1, 1, 2, 3, 3) more time(s)—6 (8, 10, 11, 13, 15, 16, 18) armhole sts dec'd total.

Cont in color stripes even along armhole edge until armhole measures about 2¼ (2¼, 2¼, 2¾, 2¾, 2¾, 3¼, 3¼)" (5.5 [5.5, 5.5, 7, 7, 7, 8.5, 8.5] cm).

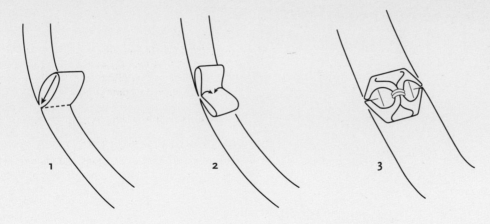

Measure 4" (10 cm) from open-ring markers and place 2 more open-ring markers into edges. Fold the band to bring the markers tog (creating an outward fold in the band for the origami flower; **Figure 1**) and pin band to right front from marker to shoulder, adjusting band length by adding or subtracting rows as necessary to end at right front shoulder sts.

Sew band from shoulder to m, then work a running st (see Glossary) through both layers of fold across band and back to seam line to secure the fold. Drop yarn to use later.

Join Shoulders

Place 18 (19, 20, 22, 22, 23, 25, 27) right front sts (including 11 band sts) onto one needle, place 18 (19, 20, 22, 22, 23, 25, 27) left front sts onto a second needle, and place 75 (77, 79, 83, 83, 85, 89, 91) back sts onto a third needle. Hold right front and back needles parallel with RS of fabric facing tog and, with MC, use the three-needle method (see Glossary) to BO 18 (19, 20, 22, 22, 23, 25, 27) right front and right back sts tog for right shoulder. BO the next 39 back sts singly, then use the three-needle method to BO 18 (19, 20, 22, 22, 23, 25, 27) left front sts tog with rem back sts for left shoulder.

Seams

With MC threaded on a tapestry needle, use the mattress st with ½-st seam allowance to sew side seams.

Origami Flower

Align outward fold line over seam **(Figure 2)**, then fold outside edges to center of band **(Figure 3)**, and whip-stitch (see Glossary) through all layers to secure.

Neckband

With A, smaller needle, RS facing, and beg at right shoulder seam, pick and knit 37 sts evenly spaced across back neck, 47 sts along left front neck edge, and 32 sts along right front neck edge—116 sts total. Place marker (pm) and join for working in rnds.

Rnd 1: [K1, p1] 40 times, k1, p2tog, k1, p2tog, [k1, p1] 15 times—114 sts rem.

Rnd 2: [K1, p1] 40 times, ssk, k1, k2tog, cont in rib to end of rnd—112 sts rem.

Rnd 3: Keeping in patt, BO 79 sts, sl 2 sts tog knitwise, k1, p2sso, BO to end.

Armbands

With MC, smaller needle, RS facing, and beg at base of armhole, pick up and knit about 88 (92, 94, 102, 102, 104, 112, 114) sts evenly spaced around armhole.

Join for working in rnds. Work k1, p1 rib for 1 rnd. BO all sts in patt.

Weave in loose ends. Steam seams, borders, and flower to set sts.

sport zip

FINISHED SIZE
About 37½ (41½, 45½, 49½)" (95 [105.5, 115.5, 126] cm) bust circumference, zipped. Cardigan shown measures 37½" (95 cm).

YARN
DK weight (#3 Light).

Shown here: Tahki Stacy Charles Cotton Classic (100% mercerized cotton; 108 yd [100 m]/50 g): #3605 olive, 11 (13, 14, 16) skeins.

NEEDLES
Body and sleeves: size U.S. 6 (4 mm): 24" (60 cm) circular (cir) and set of 4 or 5 double-pointed (dpn).
Edging: size U.S. 5 (3.75 mm): 24" (60 cm) cir and set of 4 or 5 dpn.

Adjust needle size if necessary to obtain the correct gauge.

NOTIONS
Contrasting waste yarn for provisional cast-on; F/5 (3.75 mm) crochet hook; ten markers (m), at least one of which is removable; open-ring markers; tapestry needle; 18 (20, 20, 22)" (45.5 [51, 51, 56] cm) separating zipper; sharp-point sewing needle, pins, wax and matching thread; two ⅝" (1.5 cm) buttons.

GAUGE
20 sts and 28 rows = 4" (10 cm) in St st on larger needle.

Attention to detail is the hallmark of this sporty little jacket. Alternating textures of stockinette and reverse stockinette define the vertical shaping and accent the triangle detail at the center back yoke. The lower edges of the body and sleeves are hemmed with facings (which are joined along the way) that create doubled fabric for stability and are reminiscent of well-tailored garments, complete with faux seams. The zipper provides a bold contrast to the tailored look and is topped off with a ribbed collar and a tabbed two-button closure.

BODY

With larger cir needle and using the crochet chain
method (see Glossary), provisionally CO 184 (204,
224, 244) sts. Do not join for working in rnds.

Purl 1 row, [knit 1 row, purl 1 row] 6 times for facing,
ending with a WS row.

Change to smaller needle and knit 3 rows, ending with
a RS row—1 garter ridge on RS.

Change to larger needle and purl 1 row. [Knit 1 row,
purl 1 row] 6 times.

Carefully remove waste yarn from provisional CO and
place 184 (204, 224, 244) exposed sts onto smaller cir
needle.

Joining row: Fold fabric so WS face tog and needles are
parallel with the facing sts behind the body sts, and
work *p2tog using 1 st from facing tog with 1 st from
garment body; rep from * to end of row, working the
bar between the first and last sts of facing through the
back loop for the last st—still 184 (204, 224, 244) sts.

Set-up row: (WS) P46 (51, 56, 61), k1 (faux seam st; knit
every row), p90 (100, 110, 120), k1 (faux seam st; knit
every row), p46 (51, 56, 61).

Row 1: (RS) K20 (22, 24, 26), place marker (pm), p15
(16, 17, 18), pm, k11 (13, 15, 17), pm, k1, pm, k15 (18, 21,
24), pm, p60 (64, 68, 72), pm, k15 (18, 21, 24), pm, k1,
pm, k11 (13, 15, 17), pm, p15 (16, 17, 18), pm, k20 (22,
24, 26).

Row 2: (WS) P20 (22, 24, 26), slip marker (sl m), k15
(16, 17, 18), sl m, p11 (13, 15, 17), sl m, k1, sl m, p15 (18,
21, 24), sl m, k60 (64, 68, 72), sl m, p15 (18, 21, 24), sl
m, k1, sl m, p11 (13, 15, 17), sl m, k15 (16, 17, 18), sl m,
p20 (22, 24, 26).

Slipping markers every row, rep the last 2 rows 3 (5,
5, 7) more times—9 (13, 13, 17) rows total after garter
ridge at joining row.

Dec row: (RS) K20 (22, 24, 26), sl m p15 (16, 17, 18),
sl m, k1, ssk, knit to next m, sl m, k1, sl m, knit to 3
sts before next m, k2tog, k1, sl m, p60 (64, 68, 72),
sl m, k1, ssk, knit to next m, sl m, k1, sl m, knit to 3 sts
before next m, k2tog, k1, sl m, p15 (16, 17, 18), sl m, k20
(22, 24, 26)—4 sts dec'd.

Work 7 rows even in patt as established. Rep the last 8
rows once, then rep dec row once more—172 (192, 212,
232) sts rem.

Work even until piece measures 9 (10, 10, 11)" (23 [25.5,
25.5, 28] cm) from garter turning ridge, ending with a
WS row.

Inc row: (RS) K20 (22, 24, 26), sl m, p15 (16, 17, 18),
sl m, *work left lifted inc (LLI; see Glossary) in next
st, knit to next m, sl m, k1, sl m,, knit to 1 st before

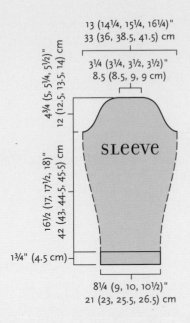

13 (14¼, 15¼, 16¼)"
33 (36, 38.5, 41.5) cm

3¼ (3¼, 3½, 3½)"
8.5 (8.5, 9, 9 cm)

4¾ (5, 5¼, 5½)"
12 (12.5, 13.5, 14) cm

SLEEVE

16½ (17, 17½, 18)"
42 (43, 44.5, 45.5) cm

1¾" (4.5 cm)

8¼ (9, 10, 10½)"
21 (23, 25.5, 26.5) cm

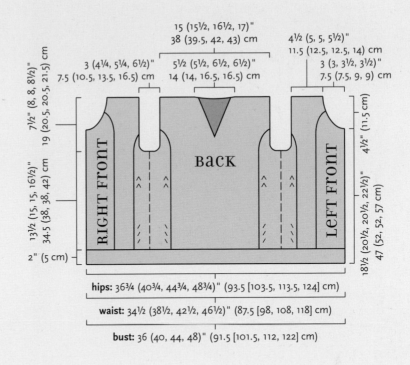

15 (15½, 16½, 17)"
38 (39.5, 42, 43) cm

4½ (5, 5, 5½)"
11.5 (12.5, 12.5, 14) cm

3 (4¼, 5¼, 6½)"
7.5 (10.5, 13.5, 16.5) cm

5½ (5½, 6½, 6½)"
14 (14, 16.5, 16.5) cm

3 (3, 3½, 3½)"
7.5 (7.5, 9, 9) cm

7½ (8, 8, 8½)"
19 (20.5, 20.5, 21.5) cm

4½" (11.5 cm)

RIGHT FRONT

BACK

LEFT FRONT

13½ (15, 15, 16½)"
34.5 (38, 38, 42) cm

18½ (20½, 20½, 22½)"
47 (52, 52, 57) cm

2" (5 cm)

hips: 36¾ (40¾, 44¾, 48¾)" (93.5 [103.5, 113.5, 124] cm)

waist: 34½ (38½, 42½, 46½)" (87.5 [98, 108, 118] cm)

bust: 36 (40, 44, 48)" (91.5 [101.5, 112, 122] cm)

next m, work right lifted inc (RLI; see Glossary) in next st, sl m,* p60 (64, 68, 72), sl m, rep from * to * once, p15 (16, 17, 18), sl m, k20 (22, 24, 26)—4 sts inc'd.

Work 7 rows even in patt as established. Rep the last 8 rows once more—180 (200, 220, 240) sts.

Work even until piece measures 13½ (15, 15, 16½)" (34.5 [38, 38, 42] cm) from garter turning ridge, ending with a WS row.

Divide for Armholes

With RS facing, k20 (22, 24, 26), sl m, p15 (16, 17, 18), sl m, k7 (8, 10, 12), BO the next 7 (9, 9, 9) sts while removing markers when you come to them for right underarm, k11 (13, 16, 19), sl m, p60 (64, 68, 72), sl m, k11 (13, 16, 19), BO the next 7 (9, 9, 9) sts while removing markers when you come to them for left underarm, k7 (8, 10, 12), sl m, p15 (16, 17, 18), sl m, k20 (22, 24, 26)—42 (46, 51, 56) sts rem for each front; 82 (90, 100, 110) sts rem for back.

Place both sets of front sts onto waste-yarn holders.

BACK YOKE

NOTE: Side panel and center back triangle shaping are worked at the same time as armhole shaping; read all the way through the following sections before proceeding.

Shape Armholes

With WS facing, join yarn at left armhole edge. BO 3 sts at beg of next 0 (2, 4, 6) rows, then BO 2 sts at beg of foll 2 (0, 0, 0) rows—78 (84, 88, 92) sts rem.

Work 1 WS row even.

Dec row: (RS) K1, k2tog, work in patt to last 3 sts, ssk, k1—2 sts dec'd.

Dec 1 st each end of needle in this manner every RS row 1 (2, 2, 2) more time(s)—74 (78, 82, 86) sts rem when decs are complete.

At the same time shape side panels as foll.

Next row: Work to 2 sts before m, p2tog, sl m, work LLI in next st, work RLI in next st, sl m, ssp (see Glossary), work to end.

Work 3 rows even as established.

Next row: Work to 2 sts before m, p2tog, sl m, work LLI in next st, knit to 1 st before next m, work RLI in next st, sl m, ssp, purl to end

Work 3 rows even as established. Rep the last 4 rows until there are 22 sts between markers.

Work even until armholes measure 7½ (8, 8, 8½)" (19 [20.5, 20.5, 21.5] cm), ending with a WS row.

Place sts onto waste-yarn holder.

RIGHT FRONT YOKE

Transfer 42 (46, 51, 56) held right front sts to larger cir needle and join yarn at armhole edge with WS facing.

Shape Armhole

At armhole edge (beg of WS rows), BO 3 sts 0 (1, 2, 3) time(s), then BO 2 sts 1 (0, 0, 0) time—40 (43, 45, 47) sts rem.

Dec row: (RS) Work in patt to last 3 sts, ssk, k1—1 st dec'd.

Work 1 WS row even.

Rep the last 2 rows 1 (2, 2, 2) more time(s)—38 (40 42, 44) sts rem.

At the same time, after 8 rows have been worked, shape side panel as foll.

Shape Side Panel

Shaping row: (RS) K20 (22, 24, 26), purl to 1 st before m, p1f&b, sl m, k1, ssk, knit to end.

Keeping in patt, rep shaping row every RS row until 2 sts rem after last marker.

Next row: (RS) K20 (22, 24, 26), purl to 1 st before m, p1f&b, remove m, ssk.

Work even in patt as established until armhole measures 7 ½ (8, 8, 8 ½)" (19 [20.5, 20.5, 21.5] cm).

Shape Side Panels

Shaping row: (RS) Knit to 3 sts before m, k2tog, k1, sl m, p1f&b (see Glossary), purl to 1 st before next m, p1f&b, sl m, k1, ssk, knit to end.

Keeping in patt, rep shaping row every 4th row until 2 sts rem before first m.

Next row: (RS) K2tog, sl m, p1f&b, purl to 1 st before next m, p1f&b, ssk.

Next row: Knit, removing markers as you come to them.

Also at the same time when armhole measures 2 (2¼, 2¼, 2½)" (5 [5.5, 5.5, 6.5] cm), ending with a WS row, shape center back triangle as foll.

Shape Center Back Triangle

Mark center 2 sts with open markers.

Next row: (RS) Working side shaping as established and keeping in patt, purl to marked center sts, sl m, k2, sl m, purl to end.

Work 3 rows even as established.

Also at the same time, when armhole measures 3 (3½, 3½, 4)" (7.5 [9, 9, 10] cm), ending with a WS row, shape center front panel as foll.

Shape Center Front Panel

NOTE: Neck shaping is introduced at the same time as the center front panel is shaped; read all the way through the following section before proceeding.

Next row: (RS) Knit to 3 sts before m, k2tog, k1, sl m, p1f&b, purl to end.

Next row: Knit to m, purl to end.

Work 2 rows even in patt as established.

Rep the first 2 rows 8 more times—11 (13, 15, 17) sts before m, 27 sts after m.

Shape Neck

Keeping in patt, at neck edge (beg of RS rows), BO 5 sts once, then BO 3 sts 1 (1, 2, 2) time(s), then BO 2 sts 3 (3, 2, 2) times—24 (26, 27, 29) sts rem.

Dec row: (RS) P1, p2tog, purl to end—1 st dec'd.

Work 1 WS row even.

Rep the last 2 rows 0 (0, 1, 1) time—23 (25, 25, 27) sts rem.

Work even until armhole measures 7½ (8, 8, 8½)" (19 [20.5, 20.5, 21.5] cm), ending with a WS row.

Place sts on waste-yarn holder.

LEFT FRONT YOKE

Transfer 42 (46, 51, 56) held left front sts to larger cir needle and join yarn at center front edge with WS facing.

Work 1 WS row even in patt as established.

Shape Armhole

At armhole edge (beg of RS rows), BO 3 sts 0 (1, 2, 3) time(s), then BO 2 sts 1 (0, 0, 0) time(s)—40 (43, 45, 47) sts rem.

Dec row: (RS) K1, k2tog, work in patt to end—1 st dec'd.

Work 1 WS row even.

Rep the last 2 rows 1 (2, 2, 2) more time(s)—38 (40 42, 44) sts rem.

At the same time, after 8 rows have been worked, shape side panel as foll.

Shape Side Panel

Shaping row: (WS) P20 (22, 24, 26), knit to 1 st before m, k1f&b, sl m, p1, ssp, purl to end.

Keeping in patt, rep shaping row every WS row until 2 sts rem after last marker.

Next row: (WS) P20 (22, 24, 26), knit to 1 st before m, k1f&b, remove m, ssp.

Work even in patt as established until armhole measures 7½ (8, 8, 8½)" (19 [20.5, 20.5, 21.5] cm).

Also at the same time, when armhole measures 3 (3½, 3½, 4)" (7.5 [9, 9, 10] cm), ending with a WS row, shape center front panel as foll.

Shape Center Front Panel

NOTE: Neck shaping is introduced at the same time as the center front panel is shaped; read all the way through the following section before proceeding.

Next row: (RS) Purl to 1 st before m, p1f&b, sl m, k1, ssk, knit to end.

Next row: Purl to m, knit to end.

Work 2 rows even in patt as established.

Rep the first 2 rows 8 more times—27 sts before m, 11 (13, 15, 17) sts after m.

Shape Neck

Keeping in patt, at neck edge (beg of WS row), BO 5 sts once, then BO 3 sts 1 (1, 2, 2) time(s), then BO 2 sts 3 (3, 2, 2) times—24 (26, 27, 29) sts rem.

Dec row: (RS) Purl to last 3 sts, p2tog, p1—1 st dec'd.

Work 1 WS row even.

Rep the last 2 rows 0 (0, 1, 1) time—23 (25, 25, 27) sts rem.

Work even until armhole measures 7½ (8, 8, 8½)" (19 [20.5, 20.5, 21.5] cm), ending with a WS row.

Place sts onto waste-yarn holder.

SLEEVES

Using the crochet chain method, provisionally CO 41 (45, 50, 53) sts all onto smaller cir needle. Divide sts as evenly as possible between 3 or 4 dpn. Pm and join for working in rnds, being careful not to twist sts.

Rnd 1: Knit.

Rnd 2: Knit to last st, p1 (seam st).

Rep the last 2 rnds 5 more times—12 rnds total.

Turning ridge: Knit 1 rnd, then purl 1 rnd, then knit 1 rnd—1 garter ridge on RS.

Change to larger dpn.

Work Rnd 2, then rep Rnds 1 and 2 five more times, then work Rnd 2 once more—13 rnds total from turning ridge.

Joining rnd: Carefully remove waste yarn from provisional CO and place exposed sts onto smaller dpn (see Notes), fold fabric so WS of fabric face tog and needles are parallel with the facing sts behind the sleeve sts, and work *p2tog (1 st from each needle); rep from * to end of rnd, working the bar between first and last st of facing through the back loop for the last st.

Work even for 8 rnds, working the seam st in garter st (alternate knit 1 rnd, purl 1 rnd).

Inc rnd: K1, work LLI in next st, knit to last 3 sts, work RLI in next st, k1, work seam st as necessary to maintain garter st patt—2 sts inc'd.

Work 7 rnds even. Rep the last 8 rnds 12 (13, 13, 14) more times, changing to cir needle when necessary—65 (71, 76, 81) sts.

Work even until piece measures 16½ (17, 17½, 18)" (42 [43, 44.5, 45.5] cm) from turning ridge.

Shape Cap

Next rnd: Knit to last 4 sts, BO 7 sts removing m when you come to it, knit to end—58 (64, 69, 74) sts rem.

Working back and forth in rows, BO 2 (3, 3, 3) sts at beg of next 2 rows, then BO 2 sts at beg of foll 0 (2, 2, 4) rows—54 (54, 59, 60) sts rem.

Purl 1 WS row.

Dec row: (RS) K1, k2tog, knit to last 3 sts, ssk, k1—2 sts dec'd.

Dec 1 st each end of needle in this manner every RS row 13 more times—26 (26 31, 32) sts rem.

BO 2 sts at beg of next 0 (0, 2, 2) rows, then BO 5 sts at beg of foll 2 rows—16 (16, 17, 18) sts rem.

BO all sts.

FINISHING

Using the wet-towel method (see Glossary), block pieces to measurements. Allow to air-dry thoroughly before moving.

Join Shoulders

Place 74 (78, 82, 86) held back sts onto larger cir needle and place 23 (25, 25, 27) held right front sts and

23 (25, 25 27) held left front sts onto another needle. Hold needles parallel with WS of fabric tog (seam will be visible on RS), use the three-needle method (see Glossary) to BO 23 (25, 25, 27) right front sts tog with first 23 (25, 25, 27) back sts for right shoulder. BO center 28 (28, 32, 32) back neck sts singly, then BO 23 (25, 25, 27) left front sts tog with rem back sts for left shoulder.

Seams

With crochet hook, use slip-st crochet (see Glossary) to join sleeve caps into armholes, matching faux side and sleeve seams and matching center sleeve caps to shoulder seams, easing in cap fullness as necessary and working from the body (not the sleeve) side of the join.

Center Front Borders

With smaller cir needle, RS facing, and beg at lower right center front, pick up and knit 90 (100, 100, 110) sts evenly spaced to neck edge, working through both layers of hem and facing. Do not join.

Knit 4 rows. With WS facing, BO all sts knitwise.

Beg at neck edge, rep for left front edge.

Neckband

With smaller cir needle, use the long-tail method (see Glossary) to CO 9 sts. Do not turn work. Cont with working yarn at right front neck, pick up and knit 24 (26, 28, 28) sts evenly spaced along right front neck edge, 27 (27, 31, 31) sts across back neck, and 24 (26, 28, 28) sts along left front neck edge, turn work and use the cable method (see Glossary) to CO 9 more sts—93 (97, 105, 105) sts total.

Knit 1 WS row—1 garter ridge on RS.

Row 1: (RS) Sl 1 knitwise with yarn in back (kwise wyb), *p1, k1; rep from * to end.

Row 2: (WS) Sl 1 purlwise with yarn in front (pwise wyf), *k1, p1; rep from * to end.

Buttonhole row: Sl 1 kwise wyb, p1, k1, yo, k2tog, work 6 sts, yo, k2tog, work to end.

Rep Row 2, then rep Row 1.

Know Your Yarn: Mercerized Cotton

John Mercer of England invented the mercerization process in 1844, but it was nearly fifty years before H. A. Lowe improved and popularized the treatment. Mercerization increases luster, strength, and affinity for dye on long cotton fibers. During the process, a chemical structural alteration causes the cell walls to enlarge and have a greater reflecting surface. Knitters enjoy the resulting softer feel and the more radiant color.

With WS facing, BO all sts as foll: Sl 1 pwise wyf, k1, psso, [p2tog, pass the last st over this one] 4 times, BO in patt to last 9 sts, [p2tog, pass the last st over this one] 4 times, p1, pass the last st over this one.

Weave in loose ends. Lightly steam-block seams to set sts.

Apply Zipper

Working on a flat surface, place closed zipper under center front garter st borders so that zipper teeth just show. Align lower edges and pin for placement. Align upper edges, ensuring that the center front borders are the same length (don't stretch) and pin for placement. Pin borders to zipper between the first two garter ridges. Unzip zipper and check WS for even application. Draw sewing thread across wax twice and and "press" thread quickly under hot iron on ironing board to strengthen the thread. With RS facing, use backstitches (see Glossary) to sew zipper in place, removing pins as you go.

Lap right collar extension over left and mark button placement on left collar extension. With yarn threaded on a tapestry needle, sew buttons opposite buttonholes.

Spray WS of button application with water to set sts.

BOLD Aran

FINISHED SIZE
About 33¾ (35¾, 37¼, 40¼, 41¾, 44, 45¾, 47¼)" (85.5 [91, 94.5, 102, 106, 112, 116, 120] cm) bust circumference.
Tunic shown measures 37¼" (94.5 cm).

YARN
Worsted weight (#4 Medium).
Shown here: South West Trading Phoenix (100% soysilk; 175 yd [160 m]/100 g): #506 turquoise, 6 (7, 7, 7, 8, 8, 8, 9) balls.

NEEDLES
Size U.S. 9 (5.5 mm): 24" (60 cm) circular (cir).
Adjust needle size if necessary to obtain the correct gauge.

NOTIONS
Waste yarn for holding sts; markers (m); two removable (open-ring) markers; size H/8 (5 mm) crochet hook; tapestry needle.

GAUGE
19 sts and 26 rows = 4" (10 cm) in St st.

For those who love cables, this top offers a contemporary twist to the expected. One large centered cable provides vertical focus as it elongates and flatters the figure. The exaggerated cable includes twisted stitches flanked by purl stitches for definition; accents of seed stitch add to the textural distinction. For a bit of extra ease, the lower center front is gently gathered. Knitted with soy tape yarn, the overall effect is quite fluid, lifting the Aran concept into a versatile category—at home in everything from dressy to casual.

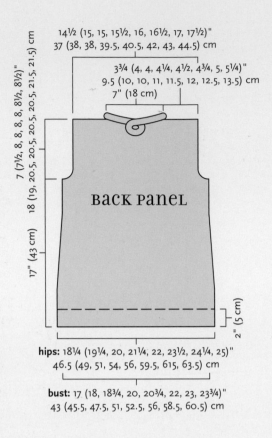

14½ (15, 15, 15½, 16, 16½, 17, 17½)"
37 (38, 38, 39.5, 40.5, 42, 43, 44.5) cm

3¾ (4, 4, 4¼, 4½, 4¾, 5, 5¼)"
9.5 (10, 10, 11, 11.5, 12, 12.5, 13.5) cm
7" (18 cm)

7 (7½, 8, 8, 8, 8½, 8½)"
18 (19, 20.5, 20.5, 20.5, 21.5, 21.5) cm

BACK PANEL

17" (43 cm)

2" (5 cm)

hips: 18¼ (19¼, 20, 21¼, 22, 23½, 24¼, 25)"
46.5 (49, 51, 54, 56, 59.5, 615, 63.5) cm

bust: 17 (18, 18¾, 20, 20¾, 22, 23, 23¾)"
43 (45.5, 47.5, 51, 52.5, 56, 58.5, 60.5) cm

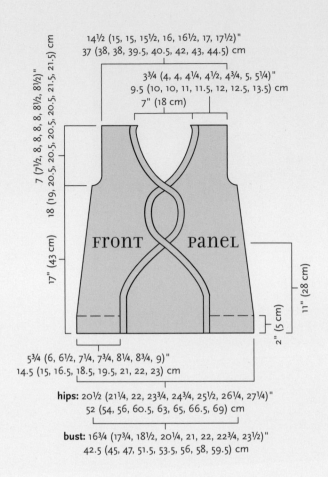

14½ (15, 15, 15½, 16, 16½, 17, 17½)"
37 (38, 38, 39.5, 40.5, 42, 43, 44.5) cm

3¾ (4, 4, 4¼, 4½, 4¾, 5, 5¼)"
9.5 (10, 10, 11, 11.5, 12, 12.5, 13.5) cm
7" (18 cm)

7 (7½, 8, 8, 8, 8½, 8½)"
18 (19, 20.5, 20.5, 20.5, 21.5, 21.5) cm

FRONT PANEL

17" (43 cm)

11" (28 cm)

2" (5 cm)

5¾ (6, 6½, 7¼, 7¾, 8¼, 8¾, 9)"
14.5 (15, 16.5, 18.5, 19.5, 21, 22, 23) cm

hips: 20½ (21¼, 22, 23¾, 24¾, 25½, 26¼, 27¼)"
52 (54, 56, 60.5, 63, 65, 66.5, 69) cm

bust: 16¾ (17¾, 18½, 20¼, 21, 22, 22¾, 23½)"
42.5 (45, 47, 51.5, 53.5, 56, 58, 59.5) cm

BACK

CO 87 (91, 95, 101, 105, 111, 115, 119) sts. Do not join for working in rnds.

Row 1: (RS) *K1, p1; rep from * to last st, k1.

Row 2: (WS) *K1, p1; rep from * to last st, k1.

Cont in seed st as established until a total of 14 rows have been worked, ending with a WS row—piece measures about 2" (5 cm) from CO.

Change to St st (knit RS rows; purl WS rows) and work even until piece measuses 4¼" (11 cm) from CO, ending with a WS row.

Dec row: (RS) K1, k2tog, knit to last 3 sts, ssk, k1— 85 (89, 93, 99, 103, 109, 113, 117) sts rem.

Work even until piece measures 8½" (21.5 cm) from CO, ending with a WS row.

Rep dec row—83 (87, 91, 97, 101, 107, 111, 115) sts rem.

Work even until piece measures 12¾" (32.5 cm) from CO, ending with a WS row.

Rep dec row—81 (85, 89, 95, 99, 105, 109, 113) sts rem.

Work even until piece measures 17" (43 cm) from CO, ending with a WS row.

Shape Armholes

BO 3 (3, 3, 4, 4, 4, 5, 5) sts at beg of next 2 rows, then BO 2 (2, 2, 3, 3, 3, 3, 3) sts at beg of foll 2 (2, 4, 4, 4, 4, 4, 4) rows—71 (75, 75, 79, 79, 85, 87, 91) sts rem.

Dec row: (RS) K1, k2tog, knit to last 3 sts, ssk, k1— 2 sts dec'd.

Work 1 WS row even.

Rep the last 2 rows 0 (1, 1, 2, 1, 2, 2, 3) more time(s)—69 (71, 71, 73, 75, 79, 81, 83) sts rem.

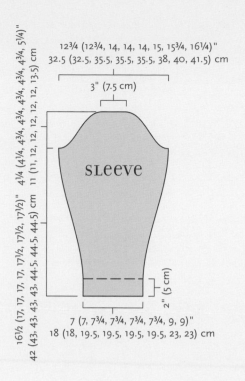

12¾ (12¾, 14, 14, 14, 15, 15¾, 16¼)"
32.5 (32.5, 35.5, 35.5, 35.5, 38, 40, 41.5) cm

3" (7.5 cm)

sleeve

4¼ (4¼, 4¾, 4¾, 4¾, 4¾, 4¾, 5¼)"
11 (11, 12, 12, 12, 12, 12, 13.5) cm

16½ (17, 17, 17, 17, 17½, 17½, 17½)"
42 (43, 43, 43, 43, 44.5, 44.5, 44.5) cm

2" (5 cm)

7 (7, 7¾, 7¾, 7¾, 7¾, 9, 9)"
18 (18, 19.5, 19.5, 19.5, 19.5, 23, 23) cm

Cont even in St st until armholes measure 6½ (7, 7½, 7½, 7½, 7½, 8, 8)" (16.5 [18, 19, 19, 19, 19, 20.5, 20.5] cm), ending with a WS row.

Shape Neck

Use removable (open-ring) markers to mark the center 19 sts.

With RS facing, knit to m, BO center 19 sts, knit to end—25 (26, 26, 27, 28, 30, 31, 32) sts rem.

Working each side separately with a different ball of yarn, BO 7 sts at neck each edge once—18 (19, 19, 20, 21, 23, 24, 25) sts rem each side.

Work even until armholes measure 7 (7½, 8, 8, 8, 8, 8½, 8½)" (18 [19, 20.5, 20.5, 20.5, 20.5, 21.5, 21.5] cm), ending with a WS row.

Place sts onto waste-yarn holders.

Front

NOTE: Side and armhole shaping are introduced while the cable pattern is in progress; read all the way through the following sections before proceeding.

CO 97 (101, 105, 113, 117, 121, 125, 129) sts. Do not join.

Row 1: (RS) [K1, p1] 13 (14, 15, 17, 18, 19, 20, 21) times, k1, place marker (pm), p1, k1 through back loop (tbl), k2, k1tbl, p1, pm, [k1, p1] 15 times, k1, pm, p1, k1tbl, k2, k1tbl, p1, pm, [k1, p1] 13 (14, 15, 17, 18, 19, 20, 21) times, k1.

Row 2: (WS) [K1, p1] 13 (14, 15, 17, 18, 19, 20, 21) times, k1, slip marker (sl m), k1, p1tbl, p2, p1tbl, k1, sl m, [k1, p1] 15 times, k1, sl m, k1, p1tbl, p2, p1tbl, k1, sl m, [k1, p1] 13 (14, 15, 17, 18, 19, 20, 21) times, k1.

Rep these 2 rows 6 more times—14 rows completed; piece measures 2" (5 cm) from CO.

Next row: (RS) K27 (29, 31, 35, 37, 39, 41, 43), sl m, p1, k1tbl, k2, k1tbl, p1, sl m, [k1, p1] 15 times, k1, sl m, p1, k1tbl, k2, k1tbl, p1, sl m, k27 (29, 31, 35, 37, 39, 41, 43).

Next row: (WS) P27 (29, 31, 35, 37, 39, 41, 43), sl m, k1, p1tbl, p2, p1tbl, k1, sl m, [k1, p1] 15 times, k1, sl m, k1, p1tbl, p2, p1tbl, k1, sl m, p27 (29, 31, 35, 37, 39, 41, 43).

Rep the last 2 rows until piece measures 4¼" (11 cm) from CO, ending with a WS row.

Dec row: K1, k2tog, work in pattern to last 3 sts, ssk, k1—2 sts dec'd.

Cont even in patt, rep dec row when piece measures 8½" (21.5 cm) and again when piece measures 12¾" (32.5 cm) from CO.

At the same time, when piece measures 6¼" (16 cm) from CO, shape center front seed-stitch panel and big cable as folls:

Set-up row: (RS) Knit to 2 sts before first m, work a left lifted increase (LLI; see Glossary) in next st, k1, sl m, p1, k1tbl, k2, k1tbl, p1, remove m, p2tog, replace m, work seed st as established to 1 st before next m, pm, ssp (see Glossary) while removing m to do so, k1tbl, k2, k1tbl, p1, sl m, k1, work a right lifted increase (RLI; see Glossary) in next st, knit to end.

Next row: (WS) Purl to m, sl m, k1, p1tbl, p2, p1tbl, k1, sl m, work in seed st as established to next m, sl m, k1, p1tbl, p2, p1tbl, k1, sl m, purl to end.

Rep the last 2 rows 13 more times.

Next row: Knit to 2 sts before first m, LLI into next st, k1, sl m, p1, k1tbl, k2, k1tbl, p1, sl m, (slip 1, k2tog, psso), sl m, p1, k1tbl, k2, k1tbl, p1, sl m, k1, RLI into next st, knit to end.

Next row: Purl to m, sl m, k1, p1tbl, p2, p1tbl, k1, sl m, k1, sl m, k1, p1tbl, p2, p1tbl, k1, sl m, purl to end.

Cable row: (RS; dec row) Knit to m, sl m, sl 7 sts onto cn and hold in back of work, p1, k1tbl, k2tog, k1tbl, p1, then p1, k1tbl, k2tog, k1tbl, p2tog from cn, sl m, knit to end—90 (94, 98, 106, 110, 114, 118, 122) sts rem; second side dec has been worked).

Next row: Purl to m, sl m, k1, p1tbl, p1, p1tbl, k1, sl m, k1, p1tbl, p1, p1tbl, k1, sl m, purl to end.

Shape Lower Middle Cable

Row 1: (RS) Knit to 3 sts before m, k2tog, k1, sl m, p1, k1tbl, k1, k1tbl, [p1f&b (see Glossary)] 2 times, k1tbl, k1, k1tbl, p1, sl m, k1, ssk, knit to end.

Row 2: (WS) Purl to m, sl m, k1, p1tbl, p1, p1tbl, k1, pm, k2, pm, k1, p1tbl, p1, p1tbl, k1, sl m, purl to end.

Row 3: Knit to 3 sts before m, k2tog, k1, sl m, p1, k1tbl, k1, k1tbl, p1f&b and pm in the center of the resulting sts, k1, p1, p1f&b and pm in the center of the resulting sts, k1tbl, k1, k1tbl, p1, sl m, k1, ssk, knit to end.

Row 4: Purl to m, sl m, k1, p1tbl, p1, p1tbl, k1, sl m, work in seed st as established to next m, sl m, k1, p1tbl, p1, p1tbl, k1, sl m, purl to end.

Rep the last 2 rows 2 more times, working 2 more sts into seed st section every WS row—12 sts in seed st section between markers.

Dec row: (RS) Knit to 3 sts before m, k2tog, k1, sl m, p1, k1tbl, k1, k1tbl, p1, work 12 sts in seed st, p1, k1tbl, k1, k1tbl, p1, sl m, k1, ssk, knit to end—86 (90, 94, 102, 106, 110, 114, 118) sts rem; third side dec has been worked.

Next row: Purl to m, sl m, k1, p1tbl, p1, p1tbl, k1, pm, work 12 sts in seed st, pm, k1, p1tbl, p1, p1tbl, k1, sl m, purl to end.

Rep the last 2 rows once more—84 (88, 92, 100, 104, 108, 112, 116) sts rem.

Work even in patt as established until piece measures 16" (40.5 cm) from CO, ending with a WS row.

Next row: (RS; dec row) Knit to m, p1, k1tbl, k1, k1tbl, remove m, p2tog, replace m, work seed st as established to 1 st before next m, pm, ssp while removing m to do so, k1tbl, k1, k1tbl, p1, sl m, knit to end—82 (86, 90, 98, 102, 106, 110, 114) sts rem.

Next row: (WS) Purl to m, sl m, k1, p1tbl, p1, p1tbl, k1, work seed st as established to next m, sl m, k1, p1tbl, p1, p1tbl, k1, sl m, purl to end.

Shape Upper Middle Cable

Row 1: (RS) Knit to 1 st before m, work LLI in next st, k1, sl m, p1, k1tbl, k1, k1tbl, remove m, p2tog, replace m, work seed st as established to 1 st before next m, pm, ssp while removing m to do so, k1tbl, k1, k1tbl, p1, sl m, k1, RLI in next st, knit to end.

Row 2: (WS) Purl to m, sl m, k1, p1tbl, p1, p1tbl, k1, work seed st as established to next m, sl m, k1, p1tbl, p1, p1tbl, k1, sl m, purl to end.

Rep the last 2 rows 3 more times.

Next row: Knit to m, sl m, p1, k1tbl, k1, k1tbl, remove m, p2tog, replace m, ssp while removing m to do so, k1tbl, k1, k1tbl, p1, sl m, knit to end—80 (84, 88, 96, 100, 104, 108, 112) sts rem.

Next row: Purl to m, sl m, k1, p1tbl, p1, p1tbl, k1, sl m, k1, p1tbl, p1, p1tbl, k1, sl m, purl to end.

Cable row: (RS) Knit to m, sl 5 sts onto cn and hold in back of work, p1, k1tbl, k1, k1tbl, p1, then p1, k1tbl, k1, k1tbl, p1 from cn, knit to end.

Divide for V-Neck

NOTE: Neck shaping is worked as armhole shaping is in progress; read all the way through the following sections before proceeding.

Next row: (WS) Purl to m, sl m, k1, p1tbl, p1, p1tbl, k1, then place these 40 (42, 44, 48, 50, 52, 54, 56) right front sts on holder to work later; k1, p1tbl, p1, p1tbl, k1, sl m, purl to end—40 (42, 44, 48, 50, 52, 54, 56) sts rem for left front.

LEFT FRONT

Dec row: (RS) Knit to 3 sts before m, k2tog, k1, sl m, p1, k1tbl, k1, k1tbl, p1—39 (41, 43, 47, 49, 51, 53, 55) sts.

Next row: (WS) K1, p1tbl, p1, p1tbl, k1, purl to end.

Rep the last 2 rows 3 (1, 1, 3, 3, 1, 0, 0) more time(s).

Keeping in patt as established, rep dec row, then work 3 rows even. Rep the last 4 rows 6 (8, 8, 7, 7, 8, 9, 9) more times—11 (11, 11, 12, 12, 11, 11, 11) neck sts dec'd total.

At the same time, when piece measures 17" (43 cm) from CO, shape armhole as foll:

At armhole edge (beg of RS rows), BO 3 (3, 3, 4, 4, 4, 5, 5) sts once, then BO 2 (2, 2, 2, 3, 3, 3, 3) sts 1 (1, 2, 2, 2, 2, 2, 2) time(s).

Dec row: (RS) K1, k2tog, work to end in patt as established—1 st dec'd at armhole edge.

Work 1 WS row even.

Rep the last 2 rows 0 (1, 1, 2, 1, 2, 2, 3) more time(s)—6 (7, 9, 11, 12, 13, 14, 15) armhole sts removed; 23 (24, 24, 25, 26, 28, 29, 30) sts rem: 5 sts for cable and 18 (19, 19, 20, 21, 23, 24, 25) sts for shoulder.

Rep the last 2 rows 3 (1, 1, 3, 3, 1, 0, 0) more time(s).

Keeping in patt as established, rep dec row, then work 3 rows even.

Rep the last 4 rows 6 (8, 8, 7, 7, 8, 9, 9) more times—11 (11, 11, 12, 12, 11, 11, 11) neck sts dec'd total.

At the same time, when piece measures 17" (43 cm) from CO, shape armhole as foll:

At armhole edge (beg of WS rows), BO 3 (3, 3, 4, 4, 4, 5, 5) sts once, then BO 2 (2, 2, 2, 3, 3, 3, 3) sts 1 (1, 2, 2, 2, 2, 2, 2) time(s).

Dec row: (RS) Work in patt as established to last 3 sts, ssk, k1—1 st dec'd at armhole edge.

Work 1 WS row even.

Rep the last 2 rows 0 (1, 1, 2, 1, 2, 2, 3) more time(s)—6 (7, 9, 11, 12, 13, 14, 15) armhole sts removed.

Cont even if necessary until armhole measures 7 (7½, 8, 8, 8, 8, 8½, 8½)" 18 (19, 20.5, 20.5, 20.5, 20.5, 21.5, 21.5] cm).

Place 5 cable sts onto one holder, place rem 18 (19, 19, 20, 21, 23, 24, 25) shoulder sts onto another holder.

BACK NECK BORDER
Return 5 left front cable sts onto needle.

Row 1: (RS) P1, k1tbl, k1, k1tbl, p1.

Row 2: (WS) K1, p1tbl, p1, p1tbl, k1.

Rep these 2 rows until border measures 12" (30.5 cm), ending with a WS row.

Place sts on holder.

SLEEVES

CO 33 (33, 37, 37, 37, 37, 43, 43) sts. Do not join.

Row 1: (RS) *K1, p1; rep from * to last st, k1.

Rep Row 1 until piece measures 2" (5 cm) from CO, ending with a WS row.

Inc row: (RS) K1f&b, k to last 2 sts, k1f&b, k1—2 sts inc'd.

Work 5 rows even in St st.

Cont even if necessary until armhole measures 7 (7½, 8, 8, 8, 8, 8½, 8½)" 18 (19, 20.5, 20.5, 20.5, 20.5, 21.5, 21.5] cm).

Place 5 cable sts onto one holder, place rem 18 (19, 19, 20, 21, 23, 24, 25) shoulder sts onto another holder.

RIGHT FRONT
Return right front sts onto needle and rejoin yarn ready to start a RS row.

Dec row: (RS) P1, k1tbl, k1, k1tbl, p1, pm, k1, ssk, knit to end—1 st dec'd.

Next row: Purl to m, k1, p1tbl, p1, p1tbl, k1.

Rep the last 6 rows 13 (13, 14, 14, 14, 11, 12, 11) more times—61 (61, 67, 67, 67, 61, 69, 67) sts.

Cont for your size as foll:

FOR SIZES 44 (45¾, 47¼)" ONLY
[Rep inc row, work 3 rows even] 5 (3, 5) times — 61 (61, 67, 67, 67, 71, 75, 77) sts.

ALL SIZES
Work even until piece measures 16½ (17, 17, 17, 17, 17½, 17½, 17½)" (42 [43, 43, 43, 43, 44.5, 44.5, 44.5] cm) from CO, ending with a WS row.

Shape Cap

BO 3 sts at beg of next 2 (2, 2, 2, 2, 2, 4, 4) rows, then BO 2 sts at beg of foll 6 (6, 8, 8, 8, 8, 8, 8) rows—43 (43, 45, 45, 45, 49, 47, 49) sts rem.

Dec 1 st each end of needle every RS row 5 (5, 6, 6, 6, 5, 4, 5) times—33 (33, 33, 33, 33, 39, 39, 39) sts rem.

BO 2 sts at beg of next 6 rows, then BO 3 sts at beg of next 2 (2, 2, 2, 2, 4, 4, 4) rows—15 sts rem.

BO all sts.

FINISHING

Using the light steam or wet-towel method (see Glossary), block pieces to measurement, encouraging lower center front seed st to gather into draping folds (do not stretch flat). Allow to air-dry completely before moving.

Join Shoulders

Place 18 (19, 19, 20, 21, 23, 24, 25) held right back shoulder sts onto one needle and corresponding 18 (19, 19, 20, 21, 23, 24, 25) held right front shoulder sts onto another needle. Hold needles parallel with RS of fabric facing tog. Use the three-needle method (see Glossary) to BO sts tog.

Rep for left shoulder.

Seams

With yarn threaded on a tapestry needle, use the mattress st with ½ stitch seam allowance (see Glossary) to sew side and sleeve seams.

Lightly steam seams from WS.

Pin sleeve cap into armhole, matching side and sleeve seams, matching center sleeve cap to shoulder seam, and easing fullness at sleeve top. With crochet hook and working from body (not the sleeve) side of the join, use slip-st crochet (see Glossary) to join sleeve to body. Lightly steam seam from WS.

Back Neck Border

Pin back neck border in place, beg at left shoulder, making a clockwise circle loop at center back neck, and cont to right shoulder.

Place 5 sts of right cable border onto one dpn and 5 sts of back neck border onto a second dpn. Cut yarn leaving an 18" (45.5 cm) tail. Thread tail onto a tapestry needle and, working from the outer neck edge with RS facing, use the Kitchener st (see Glossary) to graft the sts tog.

With yarn theaded on a tapestry needle, use vertical-to-horizontal grafting (see Glossary) to join inner purl-st edge of border to back neck. Use a running st (see Glossary) to catch underside of border at center of circle to secure the loop.

Weave in loose ends. Lightly steam seams from WS, and finger-press to reduce any bulk.

jane austen spencer

FINISHED SIZE
About 32 (36, 38, 41, 44, 46.5)" (81.5 [91.5, 96.5, 104, 112, 118] cm) bust circumference, buttoned.
Cardigan shown measures 36" (91.5 cm).

YARN
DK weight (#3 Light).
Shown here: Plymouth Grass (65% cotton, 35% hemp; 115 yd [105 m]/50 g): #9090 pale olive, 7 (8, 8, 9, 10, 11) balls.

NEEDLES
Body and sleeves: size U.S. 7 (4.5 mm): 24" (60 cm) circular (cir).

Edging: two size U.S. 6 (4 mm): 24" (60 cm) cir.

Adjust needle size if necessary to obtain the correct gauge.

NOTIONS
Two open-ring markers (m); waste yarn for holding sts; tapestry needle; five ⅝" (1.5 cm) buttons.

GAUGE
20 sts and 24 rows = 4" (10 cm) in lace patt on larger needle.
Note: To check gauge, CO 25 sts and work complete 24-row repeat; piece should measure 5" (12.5 cm) wide and 4" (10 cm) tall.

The Spencer, adapted for women's wear from a gentleman's riding jacket, debuted around 1800. Seemingly overnight, the close-fitting, waist-length, narrow-sleeved little jacket became a Regency fashion staple for women's outdoor wear. This lacy version combines the appealing proportions of a short length with a deep U-neckline for a graceful frame. The chevron lace pattern reveals colors from the layer underneath to create a soft watercolor effect. Pair it with a couple of layers of colored camisoles peeking out above and below, and accessorize with your favorite style of necklace: bold, delicate, or eclectic.

Next row: Purl.

Rep the last 2 rows once more—67 (74, 77, 80, 81, 84) sts rem.

Work even in patt until armholes measure 6½ (7, 7, 7, 7½, 7½)" (16.5 [18, 18, 18, 19, 19] cm).

Shape Neck

Mark center 29 (32, 33, 34, 35, 36) sts.

Set-up row: (RS) Keeping in patt, work to first m, join new ball of yarn and BO 29 (32, 33, 34, 35, 36) sts, work to end—19 (21, 22, 23, 23, 24) sts rem each side.

Working each side separately, BO 6 (6, 7, 8, 8, 8) sts at each neck edge once—13 (15, 15, 15, 15, 16) sts rem.

Work even in patt until armholes measure 7½ (8, 8, 8, 8½, 8½)" (19 [20.5, 20.5, 20.5, 21.5, 21.5] cm), ending with a WS row.

Place all sts onto waste-yarn holder.

RIGHT FRONT

With smaller needle, CO 39 (46, 46, 53, 53, 60) sts. Do not join.

Knit 3 rows, then purl 1 row.

Change to larger needle and work Rows 1–24 of Lace chart 2 (2, 3, 3, 3, 3) times, then work Rows 1–11 1 (1, 0, 0, 1, 1) more time, ending with a RS row—piece measures about 10½ (10½, 12½, 12½, 14½, 14½)" (26.5 [26.5, 31.5, 31.5, 37, 37] cm) from CO.

Shape Armhole

NOTE: Neck shaping is introduced while armhole shaping is in progress; read all the way through the following sections before proceeding. Maintain lace patt as much as possible when shaping armhole; if there are not enough sts to work a dec for every yo increase, work those sts in St st instead.

BO 3 sts at beg of next 1 (1, 1, 1, 2, 2) WS row(s), then BO 2 sts at beg of foll 1 (1, 2, 3, 3, 4) WS row(s)—5 (5, 7, 9, 12, 14) sts BO.

Dec row: (WS) Ssp (see Glossary), work to end—1 st dec'd.

BACK

With smaller needle, CO 81 (88, 95, 102, 109, 116) sts. Do not join for working in rnds.

Knit 3 rows, then purl 1 row.

Change to larger needle and work Rows 1–24 of Lace chart (see page 113) 2 (2, 3, 3, 3, 3) times, then Work Rows 1–12 1 (1, 0, 0, 1, 1) more time, ending with a WS row—piece measures about 10½ (10½, 12½, 12½, 14½, 14½)" (26.5 [26.5, 31.5, 31.5, 37, 37] cm) from CO.

Shape Armholes

NOTE: Maintain lace patt as much as possible when shaping armhole; if there are not enough sts to work a dec for every yo increase, work those sts in St st instead.

BO 3 sts at beg of next 2 (2, 2, 2, 4, 4) rows, then BO 2 sts at beg of foll 2 (2, 4, 6, 6, 8) rows—71 (78, 81, 84, 85, 88) sts rem.

Dec Row 1: (RS) K1, k2tog, work to last 3 sts, ssk, k1—2 sts dec'd.

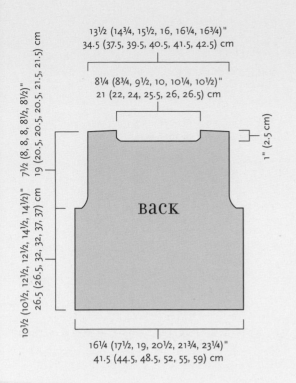

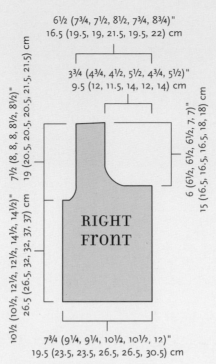

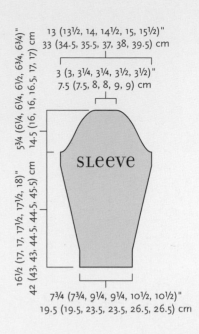

Dec 1 st at armhole edge in this manner every WS row once more—7 (7, 9, 11, 14, 16) sts total dec'd from armhole.

At the same time, when armhole measures 1½" (3.8 cm), ending with a WS row, shape neck as foll.

Shape Neck

Keeping in patt, at neck edge (beg of RS rows) BO 5 sts once, then BO 3 sts 2 (2, 2, 3, 2, 4) times, then BO 2 sts 2 (3, 3, 3, 3, 3) times—15 (17, 17, 20, 17, 23) sts BO.

Dec row: (RS) K1, ssk, work to end—1 st dec'd.

Dec 1 st at neck edge in this manner every RS row 3 (6, 4, 6, 6, 4) more times—13 (15, 15, 15, 15, 16) sts rem after all armhole and neck shaping is complete.

Work even in patt until armhole measures 7½ (8, 8, 8, 8½, 8½)" (19 [20.5, 20.5, 20.5, 21.5, 21.5] cm), ending with a WS row.

Place all sts onto waste-yarn holder.

LEFT FRONT

With smaller needle, CO 39 (46, 46, 53, 53, 60) sts. Do not join.

Knit 3 rows, then purl 1 row.

Change to larger needle and work Rows 1–24 of Lace chart 2 (2, 3, 3, 3, 3) times, then work Rows 1–12 1 (1, 0, 0, 1, 1) more time, ending with a WS row— piece measures about 10½ (10½, 12½, 12½, 14½, 14½)" (26.5 [26.5, 31.5, 31.5, 37, 37] cm) from CO.

Shape Armhole

NOTE: Neck shaping is introduced while armhole shaping is in progress; read all the way through the following sections before proceeding. Maintain lace patt as much as possible when shaping armhole; if there are not enough sts to work a dec for every yo increase, work those sts in St st instead.

BO 3 sts at beg of next 1 (1, 1, 1, 2, 2) RS row(s), then BO 2 sts at beg of foll 1 (1, 2, 3, 3, 4) RS row(s)—5 (5, 7, 9, 12, 14) sts BO.

Dec row: (RS) K2tog, work to end—1 st dec'd.

Dec 1 st at armhole edge in this manner every RS row once more—7 (7, 9, 11, 14, 16) sts total dec'd from armhole.

At the same time, when armhole measures 1½" (3.8 cm), ending with a RS row, shape neck as foll.

Shape Neck

Keeping in patt, at neck edge (beg of WS rows) BO 5 sts once, then BO 3 sts 2 (2, 2, 3, 2, 4) times, then BO 2 sts 2 (3, 3, 3, 3, 3) times—15 (17, 17, 20, 17, 23) sts BO.

Dec row: (RS) Work to last 3 sts, k2tog, k1—1 st dec'd.

Dec 1 st at neck edge in this manner every RS row 3 (6, 4, 6, 6, 4) more times—13 (15, 15, 15, 15, 16) sts rem.

Work even in patt until armhole measures 7½ (8, 8, 8, 8½, 8½)" (19 [20.5, 20.5, 20.5, 21.5, 21.5] cm), ending with a WS row.

Place all sts onto waste-yarn holder.

SLEEVES

With smaller needle, CO 39 (39, 46, 46, 53, 53) sts. Do not join.

Knit 3 rows, then purl 1 row.

Change to larger needle work Lace chart until piece measures 2½" (6.5 cm) from CO, ending with a WS row.

Inc set-up row: (RS) K1, M1 (see Glossary), place marker (pm), work in patt to last st, pm, M1, k1— 2 sts inc'd.

Work even in patt for 5 rows.

NOTE: Work sts before first m and after second m in St st until there are 7 sts, then work those sts in established lace patt.

Inc row: Knit to m, M1, slip marker (sl m), work in patt to next m, sl m, M1, knit to end—2 sts inc'd.

Work even in patt for 5 rows.

Rep the last 6 rows 11 (12, 10, 11, 9, 10) more times—65 (67, 70, 72, 75, 77) sts.

Work even in patt until piece measures 16½ (17, 17, 17½, 17½, 18)" (42 [43, 43, 44.5, 44.5, 45.5] cm) from CO, ending with a WS row.

Shape Cap

NOTE: Maintain lace patt as much as possible when shaping cap; if there are not enough sts to work a dec for every yo increase, work those sts in St st instead.

BO 3 sts at beg of next 2 rows, then BO 2 sts at beg of foll 2 rows—55 (57, 60, 62, 65, 67) sts rem.

Dec row: (RS) K1, k2tog, work in patt to last 3 sts, ssk, k1—2 sts dec'd.

Dec 1 st each end of needle in this manner every RS row 12 (13, 13, 14, 15, 15) more times—29 (29, 32, 32, 33, 35) sts rem.

BO 3 sts at beg of next 2 rows, then BO 4 (4, 5, 5, 5, 6) sts at beg of foll 2 rows—15 (15, 16, 16, 17, 17) sts.

BO all sts.

FINISHING

Using the steam or wet-towel method (see Glossary), block pieces to measurements. Allow to air-dry completely before moving.

Seams

Place 13 (15, 15, 15, 15, 16) held right back sts on one needle and 13 (15, 15, 15, 15, 16) held right front sts onto a second needle. Hold needles parallel with RS of fabric facing tog. Use the three-needle method (see Glossary) to BO the sts tog. Rep for left shoulder.

lace

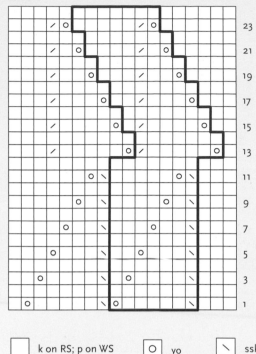

		k on RS; p on WS			$\circ$	yo			$\diagdown$	ssk
		pattern repeat			$\diagup$	k2tog				

With yarn threaded on a tapestry needle, use the mattress st with ½ st seam allowance (see Glossary) to sew side and sleeve seams.

Pin sleeve cap into armhole, matching side and underarm seams, matching center sleeve cap to shoulder seam and easing in fullness of cap. With a crochet hook, use the slip-stitch crochet method (see Glossary) to join the pieces tog, working from the garment body side.

Border

With smaller needle, RS facing, and beg at lower right front center edge, pick up and knit 55 (55, 63, 63, 73, 73) sts evenly spaced along right front edge, place marker (pm), 35 (38, 38, 38, 41, 41) sts along right front neck to shoulder seam, 46 (49, 52, 55, 56, 57) sts across back neck, 35 (38, 38, 38, 41, 41) sts along left front neck, pm, and 55 (55, 63, 63, 73, 73) sts along left

front center edge—226 (235, 254, 257, 284, 285) sts total.

Using the second smaller needle to knit back and forth on both needles to accommodate all sts, knit 1 row.

Buttonhole row: K4 (4, 4, 4, 5, 5), [yo, k2tog, k10 (10, 12, 12, 11, 11)] 4 (4, 4, 4, 5, 5) times, yo, k2tog, k1, remove m, knit to end—5 (5, 5, 5, 6, 6) buttonholes.

BO all sts kwise.

Weave in loose ends. Lightly steam-block (see Glossary) seams. Sew buttons to left front, opposite buttonholes.

Gemstone Lace

FINISHED SIZE
About 37 (41, 44½, 48½)" (94 [104, 113, 123] cm) bust circumference.
Tunic shown measures 41" (104 cm).

YARN
Sportweight (#2 Fine).

Shown here: Louet Euroflax Sport Weight (100% linen; 270 yd [247 m]/100 g): #68 steel grey, 5 (5, 6, 7) skeins.

NEEDLES
Body: size U.S. 4 (3.5 mm): 24" (60 cm) circular (cir).

Front and back lace panels: size U.S. 7 (4.5 mm): 24" (60 cm) cir.

Adjust needle size if necessary to obtain the correct gauge.

NOTIONS
Waste yarn for holding sts; open-ring markers (m); size E/4 (3.5 mm) crochet hook; tapestry needle.

GAUGE
21 sts and 30 rows = 4" (10 cm) in St st on smaller needle, after blocking.

22 sts and 23 rows = 4" (10 cm) in patt for back lace panel on larger needle, after blocking.

15 sts and 25 rows = 4" (10 cm) in patt for front lace panel on larger needle, after blocking.

This tunic-length pullover combines different lace patterns with a decorative rib balanced with stockinette stitch. A diagonal rhythm is evident in the hemlines, asymmetrical V-neck, and stitch texture, and provides adventure in knitting. The lower lace panels and sleeve cuffs are knitted separately, then sewn in place. Stitches for the long sleeves are picked up and knitted downward from the shoulders. Knitted with wet-spun linen yarn, this tunic offers exquisite drape as well as sheen when pressed and a casual matte appearance when left unpressed. Coordinate this comfortable everyday style with skirts, pants, or leggings—whatever makes you comfortable.

BaCK

With smaller needle, CO 97 (107, 117, 127) sts. Do not join for working in rnds.

Purl 1 WS row.

Cont in St st (knit RS rows; purl WS rows) until piece measures 22 (23, 24, 25)" (56 [58.5, 61, 63.5] cm) from CO, ending with a WS row.

Place sts onto waste-yarn holder.

FronT

With smaller needle, CO 97 (107, 117, 127) sts.

Set-up row: (WS) P63 (68, 73, 78), place marker (pm), p1 through back loop (tbl), k2, p1tbl, pm, p30 (35, 40, 45).

Row 1: (RS) Knit to m, slip marker (sl m), k1tbl, p2, k1tbl, sl m, knit to end.

Row 2: Purl to m, sl m, p1tbl, k2, p1tbl, sl m, purl to end.

Rep Rows 1 and 2 until piece measures 14 (15, 16, 17)" (35.5 [38, 40.5, 43] cm) from CO, ending with a RS row.

Dec row: Purl to m, sl m, p1tbl, k2tog, p1tbl, sl m, purl to end—96 (106, 116, 126) sts rem.

Next row: Knit to m, sl m, k1tbl, p1, k1tbl, sl m, knit to end.

Next row: Purl to m, sl m, p1tbl, p1, p1tbl, sl m, purl to end.

Next row: Knit to 2 sts before m, pm, k1tbl, p1, remove m, k1tbl, p1, k1tbl, sl m, knit to end.

Next row: Purl to m, *p1tbl, p1; rep from * to 1 st before m, p1tbl, sl m, purl to end.

Rep the last 2 rows 3 more times.

Next row: Knit to 2 sts before m, pm, k1tbl, p1, remove marker, k1tbl, [p1, k1tbl] to m, remove marker, p1, k1tbl, pm, knit to end.

Next row: Purl to m, p1tbl, [p1, p1tbl] to m, purl to end.

Rep the last 2 rows 2 more times.

Shape Neck

With RS facing, knit to 2 sts before m, pm, k1tbl, p1, remove marker, [k1tbl, p1] to 1 st before m, k1tbl, remove marker, p1, BO 2 sts kwise, knit to end—54 (59, 64, 69) right front sts rem. Place 40 (45, 50, 55) left front sts onto waste-yarn holder.

RIGHT FRONT

Work 54 (59, 64, 69) right front sts as foll:

Purl 1 WS row.

BO 2 sts at neck edge (beg of RS rows) 16 times—22 (27, 32, 37) rem.

Work even in St st until piece measures 22 (23, 24, 25)" (56 [58.5, 61, 63.5] cm) from CO.

Place sts onto waste-yarn holder.

LEFT FRONT

Place 40 (45, 50, 55) held left front sts onto needle and rejoin yarn at neck edge, ready to work a WS row.

Next row: (WS) K1, p1tbl, *p1, p1tbl; rep from * to m, p1tbl, purl to end.

Next row: Knit to 2 sts before m, pm, k1tbl, p1, remove m, *k1tbl, p1; rep from * to end.

Rep the last 2 rows 3 more times.

Next row: (WS) BO 2 sts in patt, *p1tbl, p1; rep from * to 1 st before m, p1tbl, purl to end.

Rep the last 2 rows 8 more times—22 (27, 32, 37) sts rem.

Work even until piece measures 22 (23, 24, 25)" (56 [58.5, 61, 63.5] cm) from CO.

Place sts onto waste-yarn holder.

JOIN SHOULDERS

Place 97 (107, 117, 127) held back sts onto one needle and 22 (27, 32, 37) held right front sts onto a second needle. Hold the needles parallel with RS of fabric facing tog and use the three-needle method (see Glossary) to BO the sts tog. BO the next 53 sts singly for back neck. Place 22 (27, 32, 37) held left front shoulder sts onto a second needle and use the three-needle method to BO them off tog with rem 22 (27, 32, 37) back sts.

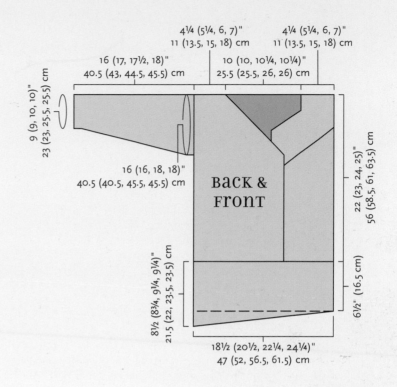

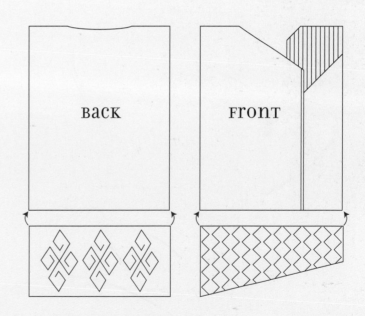

sleeves

Measure 8 (8, 9, 9)" (20.5 [20.5, 23, 23] cm) down from shoulder seam at side edges of both front and back and mark for sleeve placement. With smaller needle, RS facing, and beg at one marker, pick up and knit 83 (83, 95, 95) sts evenly spaced to other marker.

Knit 1 WS row—1 garter ridge on RS. Work even in St st for 6 rows.

Dec row: K2, ssk, knit to last 4 sts, k2tog, k2—2 sts dec'd.

Work 5 rows even.

Rep the last 6 rows 17 (17, 20, 20) more times—47 (47, 53, 53) sts rem.

Cont even until piece measures 16 (17, 17½, 18)" (40.5 [43, 44.5, 45.5] cm) from pick-up row, ending with a WS row. BO all sts.

Back Lace Panel

With larger needle, CO 81 (89, 97, 105) sts. Do not join.

Set-up row: K2, p77 (85, 93, 101), k2.

Rows 1–38: K2, begin and end as indicated for your size, work Back Lace Panel chart over 77 (85, 93, 101) sts, k2.

BO all sts.

Front Lace Panel

With larger needle, use the knitted method (see Glossary) to CO 13 (11, 11, 13) sts.

Work Row 1 of Front Lace Panel chart across 11 sts, k2 (0, 0, 2).

Next row and all WS rows: K2 (0, 0, 2), purl to end.

Keeping in patt as established, use the knitted method to CO 11 sts at the beg of the next 4 (5, 5, 5) RS rows—57 (66, 66, 68) sts.

At beg of next RS row (Row 11 [1, 1, 1] of chart), use the knitted method to CO 13 (11, 11, 11) sts—70 (77, 77, 79) sts.

Cont for your size as foll.

SIZES 44½ (48½)" ONLY

At beg of next RS row (Row 1 [3, 3, 3] of chart), use the knitted method to CO 11 (13) sts—88 (92) sts.

When CO is complete, work all WS rows as folls: K2, purl to last 2 sts, k2.

ALL SIZES

Work even on 70 (77, 88, 92) sts until piece measures about 6½" (16.5 cm) or same as back along right (short side) edge of panel, ending with a WS row.

BO all sts kwise.

Back Lace panel

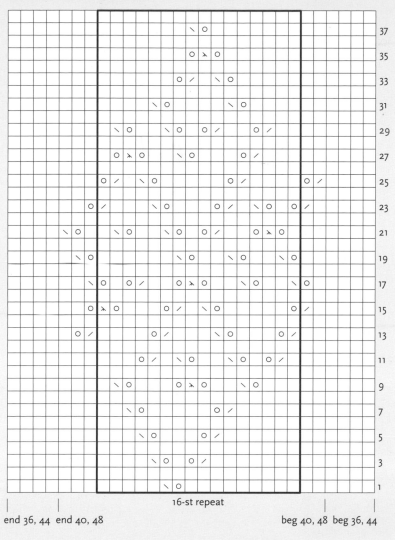

16-st repeat

end 36, 44   end 40, 48   beg 40, 48 beg 36, 44

Front lace panel

	＼	O	＼	O		O	／	O	／	11
	＼	O	＼	O		O	／			9
	＼	O	＼	O						7
	O	⋏	O	＼	O					5
O	／	O	⋏	O	＼	O				3
＼	O	＼	O		O	／	O	／		1

□	k on RS; p on WS
O	yo
／	k2tog
＼	ssk
⋏	sl 1, k2tog, psso
▢	pattern repeat

Left cuff lace panel

With smaller needle, CO 7 sts. Do not join.

Purl 1 WS row.

Row 1: (RS) Use the knitted method to CO 7 sts, *k1tbl, p1; rep from * to end.

Row 2: (WS) Sl 1 kwise, *p1tbl, p1; rep from * to last st, p1tbl.

Row 3: Use the knitted method to CO 7 sts, p1, *k1tbl, p1; rep from * to end—21 sts.

Row 4: Sl 1 kwise, *p1tbl, p1; rep from * to end.

Rep these 4 rows 2 (2, 3, 3) more times—49 (49, 63, 63) sts.

Cont for your size as foll.

With RS facing, use the knitted method to CO 8 (8) sts—57 (57) sts.

ALL SIZES
Next row: (RS) Sl 1 kwise, *k1tbl, p1; rep from *.

Next row: Sl 1 kwise, *p1tbl, p1; rep from * to end.

Rep the last 2 rows until piece measures 2" (5 cm) from last CO, ending with a RS row.

BO all sts pwise.

RIGHT CUFF
Lace Panel

With smaller needle, CO 7 sts. Do not join.

Purl 1 WS row.

Row 1: Sl 1 kwise, *k1tbl, p1; rep from * to end.

Row 2: (WS) Use the knitted method to CO 7 sts, *p1tbl, p1; rep from * to end.

Row 3: Sl 1 kwise, *k1tbl, p1; rep to last st, k1tbl.

Row 4: Use the knitted method to CO 7 sts, p1, *p1tbl, p1; rep from * to end.

Rep these 4 rows 2 (2, 3, 3) more times—49 (49, 63, 63) sts.

Next row: Sl 1 kwise, *k1tbl, p1; rep from * to end.

Cont for your size as foll.

SIZES 37 (41)" ONLY
With WS facing, use the knitted method to CO 8 (8) sts—57 (57) sts.

ALL SIZES
Next row: (WS) Sl 1 kwise, *p1tbl, p1; rep from * to end.

Next row: Sl 1 kwise, *k1tbl, p1; rep from * to end.

Rep the last 2 rows until piece measures 2" (5 cm) from last CO, ending with a RS row.

BO all sts pwise.

FINISHING

Pressing lightly, steam-block (see Glossary) pieces to measurements. Allow to air-dry completely before moving.

Seams

With yarn threaded on a tapestry needle, use the mattress st with ½ stitch seam allowance (see Glossary) to sew side and sleeve seams, working from lower edge toward underarm for each seam.

With yarn threaded on a tapestry needle, use a whip-stitch (see Glossary) to sew lace panels to lower edge of garment body as shown on page 117. Using horizontal grafting (see Glossary), join lace panels to lower edge of sleeves as shown at lower right.

Weave in loose ends. Steam-press seams from WS to set sts and reduce bulk.

Know Your Yarn: Linen

Linen may be the oldest fiber known in history, judging from Biblical references and samples found in Switzerland dating back about 10,000 years. The fiber of longevity, linen yarn is spun from the long fibers found just beneath the bark of the multi-layer stem of the flax plant. Linen was arguably the most important textile in the world before the Industrial Revolution.

Strong and inelastic, linen becomes more supple and soft to the touch with use. Woven linen fabric will crumple, but a garment knitted from linen yarn will feature all the best qualities of a crisp hand, luscious colors (due to its affinity for dyes), and comfort against the skin, all without the wrinkle.

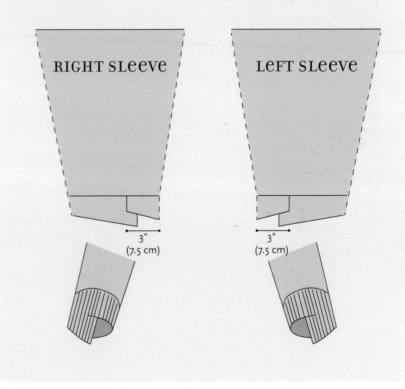

lace finery

FINISHED SIZE
About 32 (34, 36, 38, 40, 42, 44)" (81.5
[86.5, 91.5, 96.5, 101.5, 106.5, 112] cm)
bust circumference.
Shell shown measures 34" (86.5 cm).

YARN
DK weight (#3 Light).
Shown here: Tahki Cotton Classic Lite
(100% cotton; 125 yd [115 m]/50 g): #4809
teal, 6 (6, 6, 7, 7, 7, 8) skeins.

NEEDLES
Body: size U.S. 6 (4 mm): 24" (60 cm) circular (cir) plus a second needle the same
size or smaller for three-needle bind-off.
Edging: size U.S. 4 (3.5 mm): 16" (60 cm)
cir.
*Adjust needle size if necessary to obtain the
correct gauge.*

NOTIONS
Removable markers; waste yarn for holding
sts; marker (m); tapestry needle.

GAUGE
24 sts and 32 rows = 4" (10 cm) in St st on
larger needle.

This fitted shell is a balance of simple beauty
and just enough detail to hold your focus. The
asymmetrical V-neck places the vertically
patterned lace collar at an artistic angle. The
lace adds softness and visual interest to the
stockinette body. If you want a more casual
look, simply omit the lace collar for a not-so-
basic shell—just pick up the required number of
stitches around the neck, purl one round, knit
one round, then bind off all the stitches purlwise.
Try pairing this top with another sweater . . .
a knitted kimono, perhaps?

STITCH GUIDE

Lace Pattern (multiple of 6 sts + 1)

Set-up row: (WS) Purl.

Row 1: K1, *yo, k1, sl 1, k2tog, psso, k1, yo, k1; rep from *.

Row 2: Purl.

Rep Rows 1 and 2 for patt.

BACK

With smaller needle, CO 97 (103, 109, 115, 121, 127, 133) sts. Do not join for working in rnds.

Purl 1 (WS) row. Work Rows 1 and 2 of lace patt (see Stitch Guide) until piece measures 1" (2.5 cm) from CO, ending with a WS row.

Change to larger needle and work even in St st until piece measures 3½ (3½, 3½, 4, 4, 4½, 4½)" (9 [9, 9, 10, 10, 11.5, 11.5] cm) from CO, ending with a WS row.

Dec row: (RS) K1, k2tog, knit to last 3 sts, ssk, k1—2 sts dec'd.

Work 7 rows even.

Rep the last 8 rows once more, then rep dec row once again—91 (97, 103, 109, 115, 121, 127) sts rem.

Work even until piece measures 9 (9, 9, 10, 10, 10½, 10½)" (23 [23, 23, 25.5, 25.5, 26.5, 26.5] cm) from CO, ending with a WS row.

Inc row: (RS) K1, work left lifted inc (LLI; see Glossary) in next st, knit to last 2 sts, work right lifted inc (RLI; see Glossary) in next st, k1—2 sts inc'd.

Work 7 rows even.

Rep the last 8 rows once more, then work inc row once again—97 (103, 109, 115, 121, 127, 133) sts. Work even until piece measures 14 (15, 15, 15½, 15½, 16, 17)" (35.5 [38, 38, 39.5, 39.5, 40.5, 43] cm) from beg, ending with a WS row.

Shape Armholes

BO 3 (3, 3, 5, 5, 5, 5) sts, at beg of the next 2 rows, then BO 2 (2, 2, 2, 3, 3, 3) sts at beg of foll 2 (2, 4, 4, 2, 2, 2) rows, then BO 0 (0, 0, 0, 2, 2, 2) sts at beg of foll 0 (0, 0, 0, 4, 4, 4) rows—87 (93, 95, 97, 97, 103, 109) sts rem.

Dec row: (RS) K1, k2tog, knit to last 3 sts, ssk, k1—2 sts dec'd.

Work 1 WS row even. Rep the last 2 rows 0 (0, 1, 1, 1, 2, 5) more time(s)—85 (91, 91, 93, 93, 97, 97) sts rem.

Work even until armholes measures 5½ (5½, 6, 6, 6, 6½, 6½)" (14 [14, 15, 15, 15, 16.5, 16.5] cm), ending with a WS row.

Shape Neck

Mark 21 center sts.

With RS facing, knit to marked sts, join second ball of yarn and BO 21 marked center sts, knit to end—32 (35, 35, 36, 36, 38, 38) sts rem each side.

Working each side separately, at each neck edge BO 10 sts once, then BO 6 sts once, then BO 3 (3, 3, 4, 4, 4, 4) sts once, then BO 2 sts 2 times—9 (12, 12, 12, 12, 14, 14) sts rem each side.

Work even until armholes measure 7 (7, 7½, 7½, 8, 8)" (18 [18, 19, 19, 19, 20.5, 20.5] cm), ending with a WS row.

Place sts onto waste-yarn holders.

FRONT

CO and work as for back until piece measures 14 (15, 15, 15½, 15½, 16, 17)" (35.5 [38, 38, 39.5, 39.5, 40.5, 43] cm) from CO, ending with a WS row.

Set-up row: With RS facing and counting from right to left, place open-ring marker on needle after the 23rd (26th, 29th, 32nd, 35th, 38th, 41st) st; count 10 more sts to the left and place a second open-ring marker on needle—10 marked sts between markers.

Shape Armholes

NOTE: Neck shaping begins while armhole shaping is in progress for some sizes; read all the way through the following sections before proceeding.

BO 3 (3, 3, 5, 5, 5, 5) sts at beg of the next 2 rows, then BO 2 (2, 2, 2, 3, 3, 3) sts at beg of foll 2 (2, 4, 4, 2, 2, 2) rows, then BO 0 (0, 0, 0, 2, 2, 2) sts at beg of foll 0 (0, 0, 0, 4, 4, 4) rows—10 (10, 14, 18, 24, 24, 24) sts BO for armholes.

Dec row: (RS) K1, k2tog, knit to last 3 sts, ssk, k1— 2 sts dec'd.

Work 1 WS row even. Rep the last 2 rows 0 (0, 1, 1, 1, 2, 5) more time(s)—2 (2, 4, 4, 4, 6, 12) more sts dec'd for armholes; 12 (12, 18, 22, 28, 36, 36) sts dec'd total.

At the same time, when armholes measure 2½ (2½, 3, 3, 3, 3 ½, 3 ½)" (6.5 [6.5, 7.5, 7.5, 7.5, 9, 9] cm), shape neck as foll.

Shape Neck

With RS facing and working armhole shaping as necessary, work to m, BO 10 marked sts, work to end.

Place left shoulder sts on holder to work later.

RIGHT SHOULDER

Purl 1 WS row. Working armhole shaping as necessary, at neck edge (beg of RS rows), BO 6 (6, 6, 7, 7, 7, 7) sts once, then BO 4 sts 3 times, then BO 3 sts 5 times,

then BO 2 sts 8 times—9 (12, 12, 12, 12, 14, 14) sts rem when all armhole and neck shaping is complete.

Work even until armhole measures 7 (7, 7½, 7½, 7½, 8, 8)" (18 [18, 19, 19, 19, 20.5, 20.5] cm), ending with a WS row.

Place sts onto waste-yarn holder.

LEFT SHOULDER

With WS facing, return held left shoulder sts to needle and join yarn to neck edge.

Beg with a WS row and working armhole shaping as necessary, work 3 rows even.

Dec row: (RS) Knit to last 3 sts, ssk, k1—1 neck st dec'd.

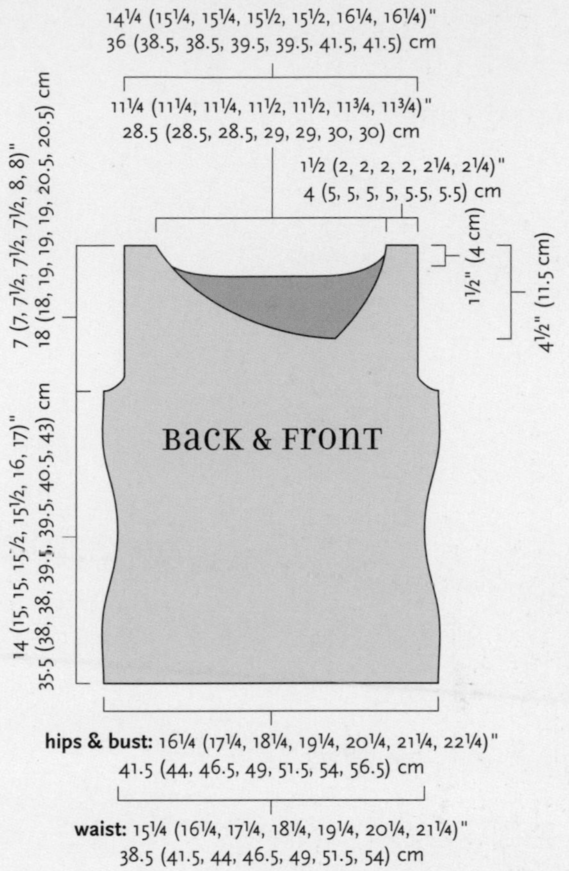

14¼ (15¼, 15¼, 15½, 15½, 16¼, 16¼)"
36 (38.5, 38.5, 39.5, 39.5, 41.5, 41.5) cm

11¼ (11¼, 11¼, 11½, 11½, 11¾, 11¾)"
28.5 (28.5, 28.5, 29, 29, 30, 30) cm

1½ (2, 2, 2, 2, 2¼, 2¼)"
4 (5, 5, 5, 5, 5.5, 5.5) cm

1½" (4 cm)

4½" (11.5 cm)

7 (7, 7½, 7½, 7½, 8, 8)"
18 (18, 19, 19, 19, 20.5, 20.5) cm

14 (15, 15, 15½, 15½, 16, 17)"
35.5 (38, 38, 39.5, 39.5, 40.5, 43) cm

BACK & FRONT

hips & bust: 16¼ (17¼, 18¼, 19¼, 20¼, 21¼, 22¼)"
41.5 (44, 46.5, 49, 51.5, 54, 56.5) cm

waist: 15¼ (16¼, 17¼, 18¼, 19¼, 20¼, 21¼)"
38.5 (41.5, 44, 46.5, 49, 51.5, 54) cm

Working armhole shaping as necessary, work 3 rows even at neck edge.

Rep the last 4 rows 7 (7, 7, 8, 8, 8, 8) more times—9 (12, 12, 12, 12, 14, 14) sts rem.

Place sts on waste yarn holder.

FINISHING

Using the steam or wet-towel method (see Glossary), block pieces to measurements. Slightly extend and pin each point of lower edge lace to encourage the scallop. Allow to air-dry thoroughly before moving.

Join Shoulders

Place 9 (12, 12, 12, 12, 14 14) right back sts onto one needle and 9 (12, 12, 12, 12, 14 14) right front sts onto a second needle. Hold needles parallel with RS of fabric facing tog. Use the three-needle method (see Glossary) to BO the sts tog for right shoulder.

Rep for left shoulder.

Collar

With smaller cir needle, RS facing, and beg at right shoulder seam, pick up and knit 76 (76, 76, 78, 78, 78, 78) sts evenly spaced across back neck, place marker (pm), 26 (26, 30, 30, 30, 30, 30) sts along left front neck edge, pm, and 62 (62, 64, 66, 66, 66, 66) sts along right front neck edge—164 (164, 170, 174, 174, 174, 174) sts total. Pm and join for working in rnds. Purl 1 rnd.

BO as foll: P29 (29, 33, 31, 31, 31, 31), BO purlwise the next 47 (47, 43, 47, 47, 47, 47) back neck sts, remove m, BO 26 (26, 30, 30, 30, 30, 30) left front sts, remove m, purl right front sts, remove m, purl rem back sts—91 (91, 97, 97, 97, 97, 97) sts rem.

Cont as foll:

Row 1: (WS) Sl 1 kwise with yarn in back (wyb), *p1, k1; rep from * to end.

Row 2: (RS) Sl 1 pwise with yarn in front (wyf), *k1, p1; rep from * to end.

Rep Row 1 once more.

Slipping first st of each row, knit 1 row, then purl 1 row, then knit 1 row.

Change to larger needle and rep Rows 1 and 2 of lace patt while slipping the first st of every row.

NOTE: The WS of the garment folds over to become the RS of the collar.

Work even until piece measures 5½" (14 cm), ending with Row 1 of patt.

With WS of collar facing, BO all sts knitwise.

Armbands

With smaller cir needle, RS facing, and beg at base of armhole, pick up and knit 84 (84, 92, 92, 96, 98, 102) sts evenly spaced around armhole. Do not join.

Knit 1 WS row. BO all sts purlwise.

Seams

With yarn threaded on a tapestry needle, use the mattress st with ½-st seam allowance (see Glossary) to sew side seams. Steam seams to set sts.

Steam collar flat, avoiding the ribbed and reverse St st turning ridge, and pinning the points as for lower edge to encourage scallops. Allow to thoroughly air-dry before moving.

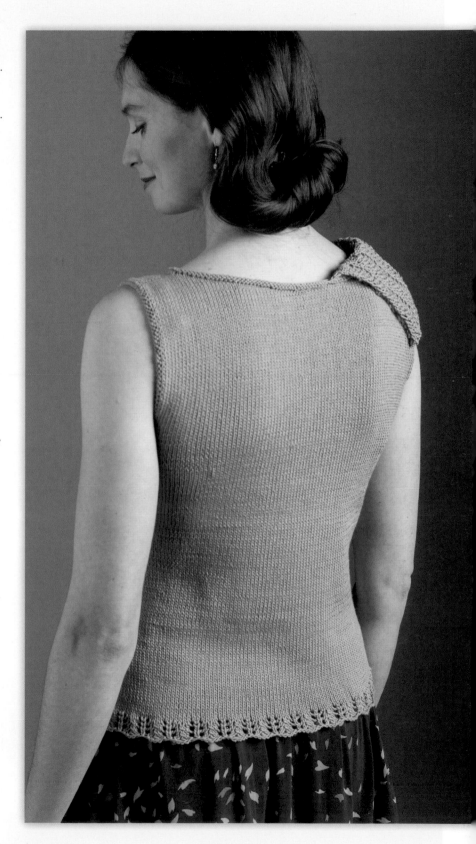

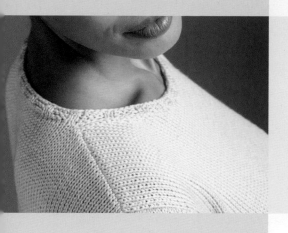

LESS-IS-MORE TEE

FINISHED SIZE
About 34 (36, 37½, 39, 41, 43, 44½, 47)"
(86.5 [91.5, 95, 99, 104, 109, 113, 119.5] cm)
bust circumference.
Tee shown measures 36" (91.5 cm).

YARN
DK weight (#3 Light).
Shown here: Cascade Ultra Pima (100%
pima cotton; 220 yd [200 m]/3.5 oz [50 g]):
#3748 cadmium yellow, 5 (5, 6, 6, 7, 7, 7,
8) skeins.

NEEDLES
Body and sleeves: size U.S. 5 (3.75 mm):
24" (60 cm) circular (cir).
Edging: size U.S. 4 (3.5 mm): 16" (40 cm)
cir and an extra needle the same size or
smaller for three-needle bind-off.
*Adjust needle size if necessary to obtain the
correct gauge.*

NOTIONS
Waste yarn for holding sts; two open-ring
markers (m); size E/4 (3.5 mm) crochet
hook; tapestry needle.

GAUGE
22½ sts and 28 rows = 4" (10 cm) in St st
on larger needle.

The basic tee is the workhorse of any wardrobe.
However, basic needn't translate to dull and
boring. With just a bit of textural interest along
the hem, cuffs, and neckline, this fashion staple
can be knitted in any color from subtle neutrals
to bold accents. Available in long, three-quarter,
short, and sleeveless options, you can enjoy this
soft cotton necessity in any season, covering the
entire spectrum of wardrobe needs from casual
to classic. Accessorized with lots of jewelry or
none, layer this top over any garment style for a
look that's uniquely yours.

STITCH GUIDE

Textured Rib *(multiple of 5 sts + 2)*

Row 1: (RS) *K2, p3; rep from * to last 2 sts, k2.

Row 2: (WS) Purl.

Rep Rows 1 and 2 for patt.

Back

With larger needle, CO 97 (102, 107, 112, 117, 122, 127, 132) sts. Do not join for working in rnds.

Work Rows 1 and 2 of textured rib (see Stitch Guide) 2 times, then work Row 1 once again.

Next row: (WS) Purl and *at the same time* dec 1 (1, 2, 2, 2, 1, 2, 0) st(s) evenly spaced—96 (101, 105, 110, 115, 121, 125, 132) sts rem.

Change to St st and work even until piece measures 14½ (15, 15, 15, 15, 15, 15, 15½)" (37 [38, 38, 38, 38, 38, 38, 39.5] cm) from CO, ending with a WS row.

Shape Armholes

BO 4 sts at beg of next 2 rows, then BO 0 (0, 2, 3, 3, 3, 3, 3) sts at beg of foll 2 rows, then BO 0 (0, 0, 0, 2, 3, 3, 3) sts at beg of foll 2 rows, then BO 0 (0, 0, 0, 0, 0, 2, 2) sts at beg of foll 2 rows, then BO 0 (0, 0, 0, 0, 0, 0, 2) sts at beg of foll 2 rows—88 (93, 93, 96, 97, 101, 101, 104) sts rem.

Dec row: (RS) K1, k2tog, knit to last 3 sts, ssk, k1—2 sts dec'd.

Dec 1 st each end of needle in this manner every RS row 2 (3, 3, 3, 2, 3, 2, 2) more times—82 (85, 85, 88, 91, 93, 95, 98) sts rem.

Cont even until armholes measure 7 (7, 7½, 7½, 8, 8, 8, 8½)" (18 [18, 19, 19, 20.5, 20.5, 20.5, 21.5] cm), ending with a WS row.

Place sts onto waste-yarn holder.

Front

CO and work as for back until armholes measure 4 (4, 4½, 4½, 5, 5, 5, 5½)" (10 [10, 11.5, 11.5, 12.5, 12.5, 12.5, 14] cm), ending with a WS row— 82 (85, 85, 88, 91, 93, 95, 98) sts.

Shape Neck

Mark center 12 (13, 13, 14, 15, 15, 15, 16) sts for center front.

Next row: (RS) Knit to m, BO center 12 (13, 13, 14, 15, 15, 15, 16) sts for front neck, knit to end—35 (36, 36, 37, 38, 39, 40, 41) sts rem each side.

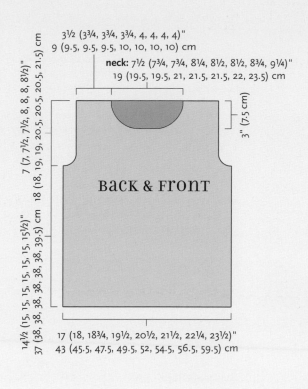

3½ (3¾, 3¾, 3¾, 4, 4, 4, 4)"
9 (9.5, 9.5, 9.5, 10, 10, 10, 10) cm

neck: 7½ (7¾, 7¾, 8¼, 8½, 8½, 8¾, 9¼)"
19 (19.5, 19.5, 21, 21.5, 21.5, 22, 23.5) cm

3" (7.5 cm)

7 (7, 7½, 7½, 8, 8, 8, 8½)"
18 (18, 19, 19, 20.5, 20.5, 20.5, 21.5) cm

18 (18, 18, 38, 38, 38, 39.5) cm

BACK & FRONT

14½ (15, 15, 15, 15, 15, 15, 15½)"
37 (38, 38, 38, 38, 38, 38, 39.5) cm

17 (18, 18¾, 19½, 20½, 21½, 22¼, 23½)"
43 (45.5, 47.5, 49.5, 52, 54.5, 56.5, 59.5) cm

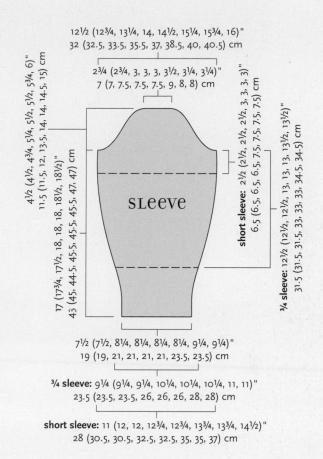

12½ (12¾, 13¼, 14, 14½, 15¼, 15¾, 16)"
32 (32.5, 33.5, 35.5, 37, 38.5, 40, 40.5) cm

2¾ (2¾, 3, 3, 3, 3½, 3¼, 3¼)"
7 (7, 7.5, 7.5, 7.5, 9, 8, 8) cm

short sleeve: 2½ (2½, 2½, 2½, 3, 3, 3, 3)"
6.5 (6.5, 6.5, 6.5, 7.5, 7.5, 7.5, 7.5) cm

¾ sleeve: 12½ (12½, 12½, 13, 13, 13, 13½, 13½)"
31.5 (31.5, 31.5, 33, 33, 33, 34.5, 34.5) cm

4½ (4½, 4¾, 4¾, 5¼, 5½, 5½, 5¾, 6)"
11.5 (11.5, 12, 13.5, 14, 14, 14.5, 15) cm

17 (17¾, 17½, 18, 18, 18½, 18½)"
43 (45, 44.5, 45.5, 45.5, 45.5, 47, 47) cm

SLEEVE

7½ (7½, 8¼, 8¼, 8¼, 8¼, 9¼, 9¼)"
19 (19, 21, 21, 21, 21, 23.5, 23.5) cm

¾ sleeve: 9¼ (9¼, 9¼, 10¼, 10¼, 10¼, 11, 11)"
23.5 (23.5, 23.5, 26, 26, 26, 28, 28) cm

short sleeve: 11 (12, 12, 12¾, 12¾, 13¾, 13¾, 14½)"
28 (30.5, 30.5, 32.5, 32.5, 35, 35, 37) cm

Working each side separately, at each neck edge BO 5 (5, 5, 6, 6, 6, 7, 8) sts once, then BO 2 sts once—28 (29, 29, 29, 30, 31, 31, 31) sts rem each side.

Dec 1 st at each neck edge every RS row 8 times—20 (21, 21, 21, 22, 23, 23, 23) sts rem each side.

Work even until armhole measures 7 (7, 7½, 7½, 8, 8, 8, 8½)" (18 [18, 19, 19, 20.5, 20.5, 20.5, 21.5] cm), ending with a WS row.

Place sts onto waste-yarn holder.

LONG-SLEEVE OPTION

With larger needle, CO 42 (42, 47, 47, 47, 47, 52, 52) sts. Do not join.

Work Rows 1 and 2 of textured rib 3 times, ending with a WS row.

Change to St st and work 6 rows even.

Inc row: (RS) K1, work a left lifted increase (LLI; see Glossary) in next st, knit to last 2 sts, work a right lifted increase (RLI; see Glossary) in next st, k1— 2 sts inc'd.

Inc 1 st each end of needle in this manner every 8th row 8 (9, 12, 10, 7, 0, 4, 2) more times, then every 6th row 5 (5, 1, 5, 9, 18, 13, 16) time(s)—70 (72, 75, 79, 81, 85, 88, 90) sts.

Work even until piece measures 17 (17½, 17½, 18, 18, 18, 18½, 18½)" (43 [44.5, 44.5, 45.5, 45.5, 45.5, 47, 47] cm) from CO, ending with a WS row.

Shape Cap

BO 4 sts at beg of next 2 (2, 2, 2, 2, 4, 4, 4) rows, then BO 3 sts at beg of foll 2 (2, 2, 2, 2, 0, 0, 0) rows, then BO 2 sts at beg of foll 2 (2, 2, 4, 4, 4, 6, 6) rows—52 (54, 57, 57, 59, 61, 60, 62) sts rem.

Change to St st and work 6 (6, 6, 6, 4, 6, 4) rows even.

Inc row: (RS) K1, work LLI (see Glossary) in next st, knit to last 2 sts, work RLI (see Glossary) in next st, k1—2 sts inc'd.

Inc 1 st each end of needle in this manner every 8th row 8 (6, 3, 4, 2, 0, 0, 0) more times, then every 6th row 0 (3, 7, 6, 9, 10, 12, 11) times, then every 4th row 0 (0, 0, 0, 0, 3, 0, 2) times—70 (72, 75, 79, 81, 85, 88, 90) sts.

Work even until piece measures about 12½ (12½, 12½, 13, 13, 13, 13½, 13½)" (31.5 [31.5, 31.5, 33, 33, 33, 34.5, 34.5] cm) from CO, ending with a WS row.

Shape Cap

Work as for long-sleeve option.

SHORT-SLEEVE OPTION

With larger needle, CO 62 (67, 67, 72, 72, 77, 77, 82) sts. Do not join.

Work Rows 1 and 2 of textured rib 2 times, then work Row 1 once more.

Next row: (WS) Purl, and *at the same time* inc 2 (1, 2, 1, 3, 2, 5, 2) st(s) evenly spaced—64 (68, 69, 73, 75, 79, 82, 84) sts.

Change to St st and work 2 rows even.

Inc row: (RS) K1, work LLI (see Glossary) in next st, knit to last 2 sts, work RLI (see Glossary) in next st, k1—2 sts inc'd.

Work 3 rows even.

Rep the inc row every 2 (2, 2, 2, 4, 4, 4, 4) rows 2 (1, 2, 2, 2, 2, 2, 2) more time(s)—70 (72, 75, 79, 81, 85, 88, 90) sts.

Work even until piece measures 2½ (2½, 2½, 2½, 3, 3, 3)" (6.5 [6.5, 6.5, 6.5, 7.5, 7.5, 7.5] cm) from CO, ending with a WS row.

Shape Cap

Work as for long-sleeve option.

Dec row: (RS) K1, k2tog, knit to last 3 sts, ssk, k1—2 sts dec'd.

Dec 1 st each end of needle in this manner every RS row 9 (9, 10, 10, 11, 11, 11, 11) more times—32 (34, 35, 35, 35, 37, 36, 38) sts rem.

BO 2 sts at beg of next 2 (2, 2, 2, 2, 2, 2, 6) rows, then BO 3 sts at beg of foll 4 (2, 2, 2, 2, 2, 2, 0) rows, then BO 4 sts at beg of foll 0 (2, 2, 2, 2, 2, 2, 2) rows—16 (16, 17, 17, 17, 19, 18, 18) sts rem.

BO all sts.

THREE-QUARTER SLEEVE OPTION

With larger needle, CO 52 (52, 52, 57, 57, 57, 62, 62) sts. Do not join.

Work Rows 1 and 2 of textured rib 2 times, then work Row 1 once more.

Next row: (Row 2 of patt) P1, [p1f&b (see Glossary)] 0 (0, 1, 0, 0, 0, 0, 0) time, purl to end—52 (52, 53, 57, 57, 57, 62, 62) sts.

Know Your Yarn: Pima Cotton

Although its origins are in Peru, pima cotton is named after the Native Americans who first cultivated it in the United States. Pima is a superior blend of extra-long fibers, prized for its exceptional softness and brilliant luster.

Rep these 2 rnds once more.

Foll patt for Row 1, BO all sts in patt.

FINISHING

Using the steam or wet-towel method (see Glossary), block pieces to measurements.

NOTE: If using the steam method, work on both right and wrong sides of the fabric.

Join Shoulders

Place 82 (85, 85, 88, 91, 93, 95, 98) held back sts onto one needle and 20 (21, 21, 21, 22, 23, 23, 23) held right front sts onto another needle. Hold the needles parallel with the RS of fabric facing tog. Use the three-needle method (see Glossary) to BO the sts tog for right shoulder. BO the next 42 (43, 43, 46, 47, 47, 49, 52) back neck sts singly, then use the three-needle method to BO rem back sts tog with 20 (21, 21, 21, 22, 23, 23, 23) left front sts for left shoulder.

Neckband

With cir needle, RS facing, and beg at right back shoulder seam, pick up and knit 42 (43, 43, 47, 47, 47, 47, 51) sts evenly spaced across back neck and 53 (52, 52, 54, 58, 58, 58, 59) sts evenly spaced along front neck—95 (95, 95, 101, 105, 105, 105, 110) sts total.

Place marker (pm) and join for working in rnds.

Rnd 1: *K2, p3; rep from *.

Rnd 2: Knit.

Seams

With yarn threaded on a tapestry needle, use a mattress st with 1-st seam allowance (see Glossary) to sew side seams.

Use the mattress st with 1-st seam allowance for sleeve rib, changing to ½ st seam allowance (see Glossary) for St st portion of sleeve.

With a crochet hook, use slip st crochet (see Glossary) to join sleeve cap to armhole, matching side and sleeve seams and matching center sleeve cap to shoulder seam, easing in fullness at cap as necessary and working from the body (not the sleeve) side of the join.

SLEEVELESS OPTION

Armhole Border

With cir needle, RS facing, and beg at base of armhole, pick up and knit 80 (80, 85, 90, 95, 95, 95, 100) sts evenly spaced around armhole.

Pm and join for working in rnds. Work as for neckband.

Weave in all loose ends. Lightly steam-block seams.

CELTIC QUEEN

FINISHED SIZE
About 32¾ (35½, 38½, 40¾)" (83 [80, 98, 103.5] cm) chest circumference, with side rib relaxed.
Top shown measures 32¾" (83 cm).

YARN
DK weight (#3 Light).
Shown here: Tahki Stacy Charles Collezione Stella (74% silk, 26% lurex; 76.5 yd [70 m]/0.88 oz/25 g): #03 champagne fizz (A), 9 (10, 11, 12) balls; #01 silver mist (B), 4 (4, 4, 4,) balls.

NEEDLES
Body: size U.S. 8 (5 mm): 24" (60 cm) circular (cir).
Edging: size U.S. 7 (4.5 mm): 16" (40 cm) cir.
Adjust needle size if necessary to obtain the correct gauge.

NOTIONS
Markers; tapestry needle.

GAUGE
22 sts and 31 rows = 4" (10 cm) in St st on larger needle.

Body-hugging with the slide of silk, this dressy top offers a nod to the Celtic influence in knitting. The extended shoulder sections create small sleeve caps, with Celtic designs showcased along the shoulders. The stand-up collar accentuated with bobbles and the ribbing along the sides amplifies the close-fit shaping and brings sophistication to the sleeveless style. Worked in a silk tape yarn infused with a subtle metallic fiber, the soft hand of this elegant top can join the party for an evening out or top a pair of jeans to amp up the casual.

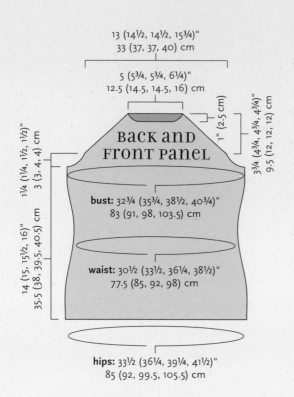

13 (14½, 14½, 15¾)"
33 (37, 37, 40) cm

5 (5¾, 5¾, 6¼)"
12.5 (14.5, 14.5, 16) cm

1" (2.5 cm)

BACK AND
FRONT PANEL

3¾ (4¾, 4¾, 4¾)"
9.5 (12, 12, 12) cm

1¼ (1¼, 1½, 1½)"
3 (3, 4, 4) cm

bust: 32¾ (35¾, 38½, 40¾)"
83 (91, 98, 103.5) cm

waist: 30½ (33½, 36¼, 38½)"
77.5 (85, 92, 98) cm

14 (15, 15½, 16)"
35.5 (38, 39.5, 40.5) cm

hips: 33½ (36¼, 39¼, 41½)"
85 (92, 99.5, 105.5) cm

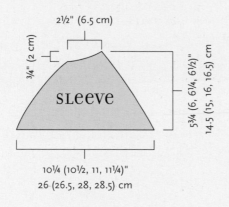

2½" (6.5 cm)

¾" (2 cm)

SLEEVE

5¾ (6, 6¼, 6½)"
14.5 (15, 16, 16.5) cm

10¼ (10½, 11, 11¼)"
26 (26.5, 28, 28.5) cm

BODY

With A and larger cir needle, CO 184 (200, 216, 228) sts. Place marker (pm) and join for working in rnds, being careful not to twist sts.

Rnd 1: K1, p2, *k2, p2; rep from * to last st, k1.

Rep this rnd 3 more times.

Set-up rnd: K1, [p2, k2] 1 (1, 2, 2) time(s), p2, pm, k78 (86, 86, 92), pm, [p2, k2] 3 (3, 5, 5) times, p2, pm, k78 (86, 86, 92), pm, [p2, k2] 1 (1, 2, 2) time(s), p2, k1.

Cont in patt as established (knit the knits and purl the purls) until piece measures 2¾ (3, 3½, 4)" (7 [7.5, 9, 10] cm) from CO.

Dec rnd: Keeping in patt, work rib to m, *ssk, knit to 2 sts before next m, k2tog, work rib to next m; rep from *—4 sts dec'd.

Work 7 rnds even.

Rep the last 8 rnds 3 more times—168 (184, 200, 212) sts rem.

Work even until piece measures 9½ (10, 10½, 11)" (24 [25.5, 26.5, 28] cm) from CO, ending with a WS row.

Inc rnd: Keeping in patt, work rib to m, *k1f&b (see Glossary), knit to 2 sts before next m, k1f&b, k1, slip marker (sl m), work rib to next m, rep from *—4 sts inc'd.

Work 7 rnds even.

Rep the last 8 rnds 2 more times—180 (196, 212, 224) sts; 14 (14, 22, 22) sts in each side rib, 76 (84, 84, 90) sts each in St st for front and back.

Work even in patt until piece measures 14 (15, 15½, 16)" (35.5 [38, 39.5, 40.5] cm) from CO, ending 3 (3, 5, 5) sts before end-of-rnd m.

Divide for Armholes

BO 6 (6, 10, 10) sts, removing m when you come to it, k2, p2 (k2, p2; p2, k2, p2; p2, k2, p2), sl m, knit to next m (front), sl m, p2, k2 (p2, k2; p2, k2, p2; p2, k2, p2), BO 6 (6, 10, 10) sts, k2, p2 (k2, p2; p2, k2, p2; p2, k2, p2), sl m, work to next m (back), sl m, p2, k2 (p2, k2; p2, k2, p2; p2, k2, p2)—84 (92, 96, 102) sts rem each for front and back.

Place 84 (92, 96, 102) front sts onto holder to work later.

BACK YOKE

Work 84 (92, 96, 102) back sts in rows as foll:

Slipping the first st of every row pwise and keeping in patt, BO 2 sts at beg of next 4 (4, 6, 6) rows—76 (84, 84, 90) sts rem.

Next row: Sl 1 purlwise, purl to end.

Dec row: (RS) Sl 1 pwise, k2tog, knit to last 3 sts, ssk, k1—2 sts dec'd.

Rep the last 2 rows once more, then work 1 WS row again—72 (80, 80, 86) sts rem.

Shape Raglan

Row 1: (RS) K1, ssk, knit to last 3 sts, k2tog, k1—2 sts dec'd.

Row 2: P1, p2tog, purl to last 3 sts, ssp (see Glossary), p1—2 sts dec'd.

Row 3: Knit.

Row 4: Rep Row 2.

Row 5: Rep Row 1.

Row 6: Purl.

Rep these 6 rows 4 (5, 5, 5) more times, then work the first two rows 1 (0, 0, 1) more time—28 (32, 32, 34) sts rem.

BO all sts.

Know Your Yarn: Ribbons

Ribbons are among the oldest decorative adornments for clothing, dating back to the birth of weaving. The demand for ribbon increased throughout the Middle Ages and Renaissance, as it traveled along the Silk Road to its final boom in the Victorian era. The textile industry classifies ribbon as narrow fabric that ranges from ⅛" to 12" (3 mm to 30.5 cm) wide.

Modern innovations have produced a ribbon yarn in small tubes that measure about ⅛" (3 mm) wide when laid flat. Knitters are the beneficiaries of these technological advances, able to see fibers with some their best characteristics augmented through this method of manufacture.

FRONT YOKE

Return held front sts onto needle and rejoin yarn at right armhole edge, ready to beg a WS row. Work back and forth in rows as foll:

Slipping the first st of every row pwise and keeping in patt, BO 2 sts at beg of next 4 (4, 6, 6) rows—76 (84, 84, 90) sts rem.

Next row: Sl 1 pwise, purl to end.

Dec row: (RS) Sl 1 purlwise, k2tog, knit to last 3 sts, ssk, k1—2 sts dec'd.

Rep last 2 rows once, then work 1 WS row again—72 (80, 80, 86) sts rem.

Shape Raglan

Work Rows 1–6 of raglan shaping as for back 4 (5, 5, 5) times—40 (40, 40, 46) sts rem.

Shape Neck

Mark center 16 (16, 16, 22) sts for neck.

Cont working raglan decs as established, divide for neck as foll:

With RS facing, sl 1, ssk, k9, BO center 16 (16, 16, 22) sts, k9, k2tog, k1—11 sts rem each side.

RIGHT FRONT

Row 1: (WS) P1, p2tog, purl to end—10 sts rem.

Row 2: (RS) BO 5 sts, knit to end—5 sts rem.

Row 3: P1, p2tog, purl to end—4 sts rem.

Row 4: K1, k2tog, k1—3 sts rem.

P3tog, cut yarn, and draw tail through last loop to secure.

LEFT FRONT

Return 11 left front sts to needle and join yarn to neck edge in preparation to work a WS row.

Row 1: (WS) BO 5 sts pwise, purl to last 3 sts, ssp, p1—5 sts rem.

Row 2: Knit.

Row 3: Purl to last 3 sts, ssp, p1—4 sts rem.

Row 4: K1, ssk, k1—3 sts rem.

Sssp (see Glossary), cut yarn, and draw tail through last loop to secure.

SLEEVES

With B, CO 56 (58, 60, 62) sts.

Omitting decreases (work these sts as k1 insead), work rows 7–8, (5–6, 3–4, 1–2) of Cable chart.

Beg with Row 9 (7, 5, 3), work through Row 44 of Cable chart—14 sts rem.

Work right and left sleeves differently as foll.

RIGHT SLEEVE

Cont following Rows 45–49 of Cable chart, at neck edge (beg of RS rows), BO 5 sts 2 times, then BO 4 sts once.

LEFT SLEEVE

Following Rows 45–49 of Left Sleeve chart, at neck edge (beg of WS rows), BO 5 sts 2 times, then BO 4 sts once.

FINISHING

Using the wet-towel method (see Glossary), block pieces to measurements.

Join Sleeves to Front and Back

Align neck edge of sleeves with front and back of garment, lower edge of sleeve to St st edge of front and back at underarm, and pin in place. With yarn threaded on a tapestry needle, use a mattress st with 1-st seam allowance (see Glossary) to sew raglan seams.

Neckband

With B, smaller cir needle, RS facing, and beg at right back/sleeve seam, pick up and knit 26 (30, 30, 34) sts evenly spaced across back neck, 14 sts along left sleeve, 34 (34, 34, 38) sts along front neck, and 14 sts along right sleeve—88 (92, 92, 100) sts total.

Pm and join for working in rnds.

Purl 1 rnd.

Change to A and knit 1 rnd, then purl 1 rnd.

Change to B and knit 1 rnd.

Next rnd: *K2, p2; rep from *.

Rep the last rnd once more.

Bobble rnd: *K2, p1, lift the ladder between needles from front, then knit into the front, back, front, back, and front of this ladder (5 sts made from ladder), turn work, p5, turn work, k5, pass the 2nd, 3rd, 4th, and 5th sts over the first and off the needle, p1; rep from *—22 (23, 23, 25) bobbles made; 110 (115, 115, 125) sts.

Next rnd: *K2, p2tog, p1; rep from *—88 (92, 92, 100) sts rem.

BO all sts in patt.

Weave in loose ends. Lightly mist seams to set sts.

LEFT SLEEVE

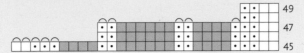

CABLE

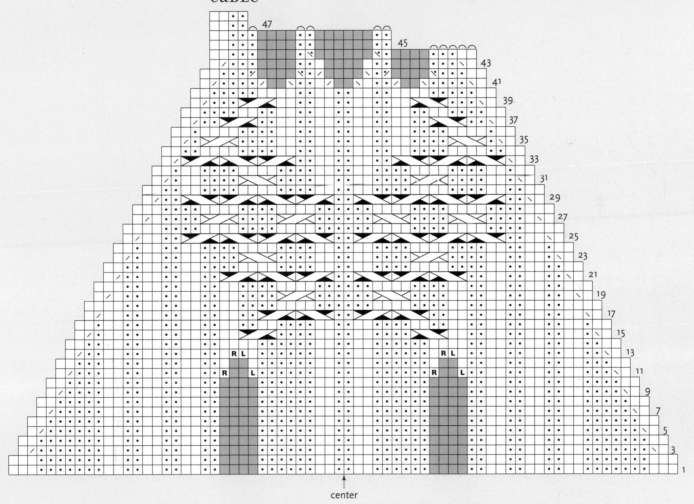

center

	k on RS; p on WS		k2tog on RS; p2tog on WS		sl 2 sts onto cn, hold in back, k2, k2 from cn
•	p on RS; k on WS		ssk on RS; ssp on WS		sl 2 sts onto cn, hold in front, k2, k2 from cn
R	right lifted inc		p2tog on RS; k2tog on WS		sl 2 sts onto cn, hold in back, k2, p2 from cn
L	left lifted inc		ssp on RS; ssk on WS		sl 2 sts onto cn, hold in front, p2, k2 from cn
	no stitch	⌒	bind off 1 st		

tesserae

FINISHED SIZE
About 33 (36, 39, 41½, 44½, 47½)" (84
[91.5, 99, 105.5, 113, 120.5] cm) bust circumference.
Tee shown measures 33" (84 cm).

YARN
DK weight (#3 Light).
Shown here: Patons Grace (100% mercer-
ized cotton; 136 yd [125 m]/50 g): #1104
black (A), 4 (4, 5, 5, 6, 6) balls; #1102 white
(B), 4 (4, 5, 5, 6, 6) balls.

NEEDLES
Body and sleeves: size U.S. 6 (4 mm): 24"
(60 cm) circular (cir) and extra needle
of same size or smaller for three-needle
bind-off.
Edging: size U.S. 4 (3.5 mm): 16" and 24"
(40 cm and 60 cm) cir.
*Adjust needle size if necessary to obtain the
correct gauge.*

NOTIONS
Waste-yarn stitch holders; open-ring markers (m); size E/4 (3.5 mm) crochet hook;
tapestry needle.

GAUGE
22.5 sts and 42 rows = 4" (10 cm) in slip-st
patt on larger needle.

Tesserae are the small pieces of stone or glass used in ancient mosaics. Stone was used primarily for floors, while glass of every hue was popular for wall and vault mosaics in Early Christian and Byzantine churches. The pebbly texture in this slip-stitch tee is reminiscent of those opulent mosaics. Either short sleeved or sleeveless, this top provides unexpected color play—dramatic in black and white, but other color pairs can add brilliant wardrobe accents. Try soft yellow and orange, kiwi and turquoise, cinnamon and eggplant; the combinations are endless!

STITCH GUIDE

Slip-Stitch Pattern *(multiple of 4 sts + 1)*

Row 1: (WS) With A, purl.

Row 2: (RS) With B, k1, *sl 1 purlwise with yarn in back (pwise wyb), sl 1 purlwise with yarn in front (pwise wyf), sl 1 pwise wyb, k1; rep from *.

Row 3: With B, p1, *sl 3 pwise wyb, yo, p1; rep from *.

Row 4: With A, knit and *at the same time* drop all yarnovers to front of work.

Row 5: With A, purl.

Row 6: With B, k1, *sl 1 pwise wyb, insert needle from front under the loose strand and knit next st tog with this strand, sl 1 pwise wyb, k1; rep from *.

Row 7: With B, p1, *sl 1 pwise wyf, p1, sl 1 pwise wyf, k1; rep from * to last 4 sts, [sl 1 pwise wyf, p1] 2 times.

Row 8: With A, knit.

Row 9: With A, purl.

Row 10: With B, k1, *sl 1 pwise wyf, k1; rep from *.

Rows 11–20: Rep Rows 1–10, reversing colors.

Rep Rows 1–20 for patt.

BACK

With A and smaller needle, CO 93 (101, 109, 117, 125, 133) sts. Do not join for knitting in rnds.

Knit 5 rows.

Change to larger needle and work Rows 1–20 of slip-st patt (see Stitch Guide) 6 (6, 7, 7, 8, 8) times, then work Rows 1–7 (17, 7, 17, 7, 7) once more—piece measures about 12½ (13½, 14½, 15½, 16½, 16½)" (31.5 [34.5, 37, 39.5, 42, 42] cm) from CO.

Shape Armholes

BO 4 sts at beg of next 2 (2, 2, 4, 4, 6) rows—85 (93, 101, 101, 109, 109) sts rem.

Keeping in patt, dec 1 st each end of needle every RS row 2 (4, 6, 6, 6, 6) times—81 (85, 89, 89, 97, 97) sts rem.

Cont even in patt until armholes measure about 7 (7, 8, 8, 8, 8)" (18 [18, 20.5, 20.5, 20.5, 20.5] cm), ending with Row 17 (7, 7, 17, 7, 7) of patt.

Place sts onto waste-yarn holder.

FRONT

CO and work as for back until armholes measure 4 (4, 5, 5, 5, 5)" (10 [10, 12.5, 12.5, 12.5, 12.5] cm), ending with a WS row—81 (85, 89, 89, 97, 97) sts.

Divide for Front Neck

With open-ring markers, mark center 13 (13, 13, 13, 15, 15) sts.

With RS facing and keeping in patt, work to first m, BO center 13 (13, 13, 13, 15, 15) sts, work to end—34 (36, 38, 38, 41, 41) sts rem each side.

Keeping in patt and working each side separately, at each neck edge BO 5 sts once, then BO 2 sts once, then dec 1 st every right side row 8 times—19 (21, 23, 23, 26, 26) sts rem each side.

Work even until armholes measure same as for back, ending with Row 17 (7, 7, 17, 7, 7) of patt.

Place sts onto waste-yarn holders.

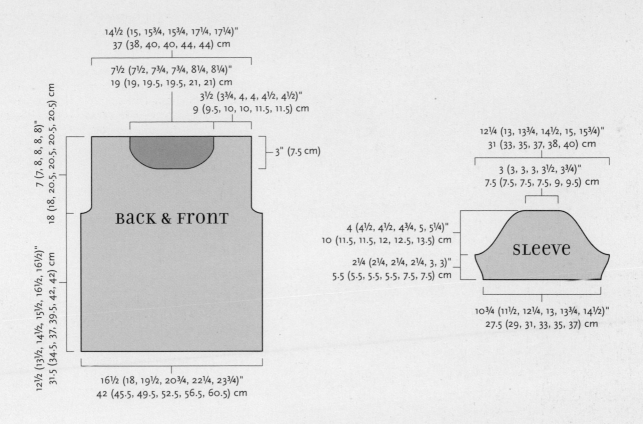

14½ (15, 15¾, 15¾, 17¼, 17¼)"
37 (38, 40, 40, 44, 44) cm

7½ (7½, 7¾, 7¾, 8¼, 8¼)"
19 (19, 19.5, 19.5, 21, 21) cm

3½ (3¾, 4, 4, 4½, 4½)"
9 (9.5, 10, 10, 11.5, 11.5) cm

3" (7.5 cm)

7 (7, 8, 8, 8, 8)"
18 (18, 20.5, 20.5, 20.5, 20.5) cm

back & front

12½ (13½, 14½, 15½, 16½, 16½)"
31.5 (34.5, 37, 39.5, 42, 42) cm

16½ (18, 19½, 20¾, 22¼, 23¾)"
42 (45.5, 49.5, 52.5, 56.5, 60.5) cm

12¼ (13, 13¾, 14½, 15, 15¾)"
31 (33, 35, 37, 38, 40) cm

3 (3, 3, 3, 3½, 3¾)"
7.5 (7.5, 7.5, 7.5, 9, 9.5) cm

4 (4½, 4½, 4¾, 5, 5¼)"
10 (11.5, 11.5, 12, 12.5, 13.5) cm

2¼ (2¼, 2¼, 2¼, 3, 3)"
5.5 (5.5, 5.5, 5.5, 7.5, 7.5) cm

sleeve

10¾ (11½, 12¼, 13, 13¾, 14½)"
27.5 (29, 31, 33, 35, 37) cm

sleeves

With A and smaller needle, CO 61 (65, 69, 73, 77, 81) sts. Do not join.

Knit 5 rows.

Change to larger needle and work WS Row 1 of slip-st patt.

Inc row: (RS; Row 2 of patt) K1, M1 (see Glossary), cont in patt to last st, M1, k1—63 (67, 71, 75, 79, 83) sts.

Next row: (Row 3 of patt) P1, cont in patt, working inc'd sts in St st, p1.

Cont in patt as established, rep Inc row every 4th row 3 more times—69 (73, 77, 81, 85, 89) sts.

Work even in patt until piece measures about 2¼ (2¼, 2¼, 2¼, 3, 3)" (5.5 [5.5, 5.5, 5.5, 7.5, 7.5] cm) from CO, ending with Row 17 (17, 17, 17, 7, 7) of patt.

Shape Cap

Keeping in patt, BO 4 sts at beg of next 2 rows, then BO 2 sts at beg of foll 2 (2, 2, 4, 4, 4) rows—57 (61, 65, 65, 69, 73) sts rem.

Dec 1 st at each end of needle every RS row 18 (20, 20, 20, 21, 22) times—21 (21, 25, 25, 27, 29) sts rem.

BO 2 sts at beg of next 2 (2, 4, 4, 4, 4) rows—17 (17, 17, 17, 19, 21) sts rem.

BO all sts.

Seams

With yarn threaded on a tapestry needle, use the mattress st with ½-st seam allowance (see Glossary) to sew side and sleeve seams.

With a crochet hook, use slip st crochet (see Glossary) to join sleeve cap to armhole, matching side and sleeve seams and matching center sleeve cap to shoulder seam, easing in fullness at cap as necessary and working from the body (not the sleeve) side of the join.

Neckband

With A, shorter cir needle, and beg at left front shoulder seam, pick up and knit 68 (68, 68, 68, 70, 70) sts evenly spaced around front neck and 41 (41, 41, 41, 43, 43) sts across back neck—109 (109, 109, 109, 113, 113) sts total.

Place marker and join for working in rnds.

[Purl 1 rnd, knit 1 rnd] 2 times.

BO all sts pwise.

SLEEVELESS OPTION

Armhole Border

With shorter cir needle, RS facing, and beg at base of armhole, pick up and knit 80 (86, 98, 106, 106, 112) sts evenly spaced around armhole.

Place marker and join for working in rnds.

[Purl 1 rnd, knit 1 rnd] 2 times.

BO all sts pwise.

Weave in loose ends. Lightly steam-block seams to minimize bulk.

FINISHING

Steam-block (see Glossary) pieces to measurements, working from both right and wrong sides.

Join Shoulders

Place 81 (85, 89, 89, 97, 97) held back sts onto one needle and 19 (21, 23, 23, 26, 26) held right front and 19 (21, 23, 23, 26, 26) held left front sts onto another needle. With RS tog, use the three-needle method (see Glossary) to BO 19 (21, 23, 23, 26, 26) right front and 19 (21, 23, 23, 26, 26) right back sts tog for right shoulder. BO the next 43 (43, 43, 43, 45, 45) back neck sts singly, then BO rem left front sts tog with rem back sts for left shoulder.

Glossary
Abbreviations

beg(s)	begin(s); beginning
BO	bind off
cir	circular
cm	centimeter(s)
cn	cable needle
CO	cast on
cont	continue(s); continuing
dec(s)('d)	decrease(s); decreasing; decreased
dpn	double-pointed needles
foll	follow(s); following
g	gram(s)
inc(s)('d)	increase(s); increasing; increase(d)
k	knit
k1f&b	knit into the front and back of same stitch
k2tog	knit 2 stitches together
k3tog	knit 3 stitches together
kwise	knitwise, as if to knit
m	marker(s)
mm	millimeter(s)
M1	make one (increase)
oz	ounce
p	purl
p1f&b	purl into front and back of same stitch
p2tog	purl 2 stitches together
patt(s)	pattern(s)
pm	place marker
psso	pass slipped stitch over
pwise	purlwise; as if to purl
rem	remain(s); remaining
rep	repeat(s); repeating
Rev St st	reverse stockinette stitch
rnd(s)	round(s)
RS	right side
sl	slip
sl st	slip st (slip 1 stitch purlwise unless otherwise indicated)
ssk	slip, slip, knit (decrease)
st(s)	stitch(es)
St st	stockinette stitch
tbl	through back loop
tog	together
WS	wrong side
wyb	with yarn in back
wyf	with yarn in front
yd	yard(s)
yo	yarnover
*	repeat starting point
* *	repeat all instructions between asterisks
( )	alternate measurements and/or instructions
[ ]	work instructions as a group a specified number of times

BIND-OFFS

Sloped Bind-Off

Use this method when working a series of bind-offs in groups, as for shaped shoulders.

On the row preceding the bind-off row, do not work the last stitch. Turn the work (there will be one stitch on the right needle tip), bring the working yarn to the back and slip the first stitch on the left needle purlwise (**Figure 1**). Use the left needle tip to lift the unworked stitch over the slipped stitch and off the needle (**Figure 2**)—one stitch bound off. Use the standard method to bind off the rest of the stitches in the group, then repeat from * for each group.

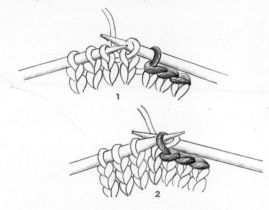

Standard Bind-Off

Knit the first stitch, *knit the next stitch (two stitches on right needle), insert left needle tip into first stitch on right needle (**Figure 1**) and lift this stitch up and over the second stitch (**Figure 2**) and off the needle (**Figure 3**). Repeat from * for the desired number of stitches.

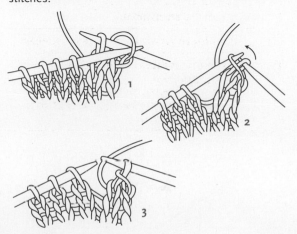

Three-Needle Bind-Off

Place the stitches to be joined onto two separate needles and hold the needles parallel with the right sides of knitting facing together. Insert a third needle into the first stitch on each of two needles (**Figure 1**) and knit them together (**Figure 2**), *knit the next stitch on each needle the same way, then use the left needle tip to lift the first stitch over the second and off the needle (**Figure 3**). Repeat from * until no stitches remain on first two needles. Cut yarn and pull tail through last stitch to secure.

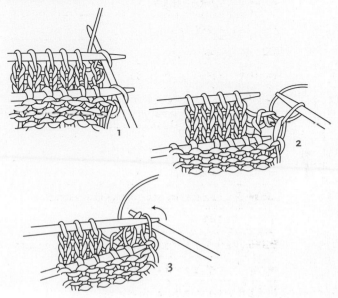

BLOCKING

Mist Blocking

Generously spray both right and wrong sides with water. Lay on a flat surface, pin to desired dimensions, if necessary, and let dry completely before moving.

Steam Blocking

Pin the pieces to be blocked to a blocking surface. Hold an iron set on the steam setting ½" (1.5 cm) above the knitted surface and direct the steam over the entire surface (except ribbing). You can get similar results by placing wet cheesecloth on top of the knitted surface and touching it lightly with a dry iron. Lift and set down the iron gently; do not use a pushing motion.

Wet-Towel Blocking

Run a large bath or beach towel (or two towels for larger projects) through the rinse/spin cycle of a washing machine. Roll the knitted pieces in the wet towel(s), place the roll in a plastic bag, and leave overnight so that the knitted pieces become uniformly damp. Pin the damp pieces to a blocking surface and let air-dry thoroughly.

BUTTONHOLES

One-Row Buttonhole

With RS facing, bring yarn to front, slip the next stitch purlwise, return yarn to the back, *slip the next stitch purlwise, pass the first slipped stitch over the second slipped stitch and off the needle; repeat from * two more times **(Figure 1)**. Slip the last stitch on the right needle tip to the left needle tip and turn the work so that the wrong side is facing. **With yarn in back, insert right needle tip between the first two stitches on the left needle tip **(Figure 2)**, draw through a loop and place it on the left needle]; rep from ** three more times, then turn the work so the right side is facing. With yarn in back, slip the first stitch and lift the extra cast-on stitch over the slipped stitch **(Figure 3)** and off the needle to complete the buttonhole.

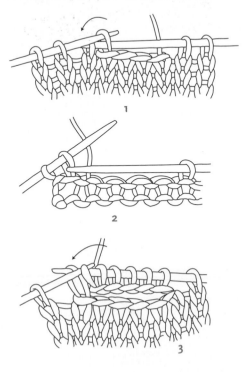

CAST-ONS

Backward-Loop Cast-On

*Loop working yarn and place it on needle backward so that it doesn't unwind. Repeat from *.

Cable Cast-On

If there are no stitches on the needles, make a slipknot of working yarn and place it on the left needle, then use the knitted method to cast-on one more stitch—two stitches on needle. When there are at least two stitches on the left needle, hold needle with working yarn in your left hand. *Insert right needle between the first two stitches on left needle **(Figure 1)**, wrap yarn around needle as if to knit, draw yarn through **(Figure 2)**, and place new loop on left needle **(Figure 3)** to form a new stitch. Repeat from * for the desired number of stitches, always working between the first two stitches on the left needle.

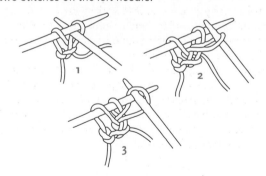

Crochet Chain Provisional Cast-On

With waste yarn and crochet hook, make a loose crochet chain (see page 149) about four stitches more than you need to cast on. With knitting needle, working yarn, and beginning two stitches from end of chain, pick up and knit one stitch through the back loop of each crochet chain **(Figure 1)** for desired number of stitches. When you're ready to work in the opposite direction, pull out the crochet chain to expose live stitches **(Figure 2)**.

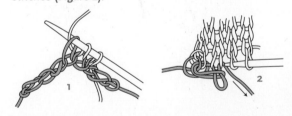

Knitted Cast-On

If there are no stitches on the needles, make a slipknot of working yarn and place it on the left needle. When there is at least one stitch on the left needle, *use the right needle to knit the first stitch (or slipknot) on left needle (Figure 1) and place new loop onto left needle to form a new stitch (Figure 2). Repeat from * for the desired number of stitches, always working into the last stitch made.

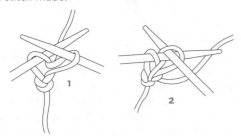

Long-Tail (Continental) Cast-On

Leaving a long tail (about ½" [1.3 cm] for each stitch to be cast on), make a slipknot and place on right needle. Place thumb and index finger of your left hand between the yarn ends so that working yarn is around your index finger and tail end is around your thumb; secure the yarn ends with your other fingers. Hold your palm upwards, making a V of yarn (Figure 1). *Bring needle up through loop on thumb (Figure 2), catch first strand around index finger, and go back down through loop on thumb (Figure 3). Drop loop off thumb and, placing thumb back in V configuration, tighten resulting stitch on needle (Figure 4). Repeat from * for the desired number of stitches.

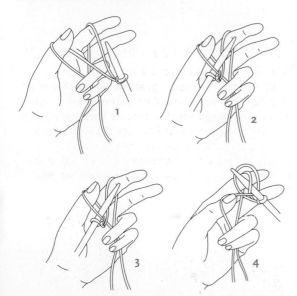

CROCHET

Crochet Chain (ch)

Make a slipknot and place it on crochet hook if there isn't a loop already on the hook. *Yarn over hook and draw through loop on hook. Repeat from * for the desired number of stitches. To fasten off, cut yarn and draw end through last loop formed.

Single Crochet (sc)

*Insert hook into the second chain from the hook (or the next stitch), yarn over hook and draw through a loop, yarn over hook (Figure 1), and draw it through both loops on hook (Figure 2). Repeat from * for the desired number of stitches.

decreases

Slip, Slip, Knit (ssk)

Slip two stitches individually knitwise **(Figure 1)**. Insert left needle tip into the front of these two slipped stitches, and use the right needle to knit them together through their back loops **(Figure 2)**.

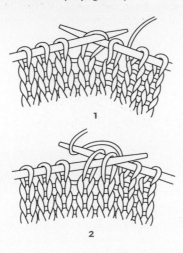

Slip, Slip, Purl (ssp)

Holding yarn in front, slip two stitches individually knitwise **(Figure 1)**, then slip these two stitches back onto left needle (they will be twisted on the needle) and purl them together through their back loops **(Figure 2)**.

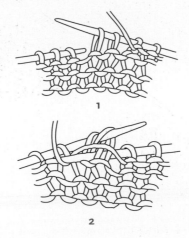

EMBROIDERY

Crochet Chain Stitch

Holding the yarn under the background, insert crochet hook through the center of a knitted stitch, pull up a loop, *insert hook into the center of the next stitch to the right, pull up a second loop through the first loop on the hook. Repeat from *.

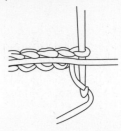

Daisy Stitch

*Bring threaded needle out of knitted background from back to front, form a short loop, then insert needle into background where it came out. Keeping the loop under the needle, bring the needle back out of the background a short distance away **(Figure 1)**, pull loop snug, and insert needle into fabric on far side of loop.

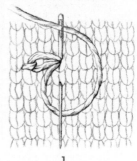

Fly Stitch

Working from top to bottom, *bring threaded needle out from back to front at the desired placement; insert needle a short distance to the right to form a loop, then insert needle a short distance below, holding the loop below the tip of the needle. Insert needle to WS a short distance below loop for stem. Rep from *.

French Knot

Bring threaded needle out of knitted background from back to front, wrap yarn around needle one to three times, and use your thumb to hold the wraps in place while you insert needle into background a short distance from where it came out. Pull the needle through the wraps into the background.

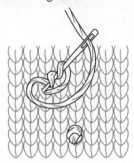

Running Stitch

Bring threaded needle in and out of background to form a dashed line.

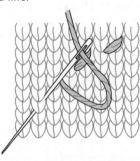

I-CORD

(also called Knit-Cord)

This is worked with two double-pointed needles. Cast on the desired number of stitches (usually 3 to 4). Knit across these stitches, then *without turning the needle, slide stitches to other end of needle, pull the yarn around the back, and knit the stitches as usual. Repeat from * for desired length.

increases

Bar Increase

KNITWISE (K1F&B)

Knit into a stitch but leave the stitch on the left needle (**Figure 1**), then knit through the back loop of the same stitch (**Figure 2**) and slip the original stitch off the needle (**Figure 3**).

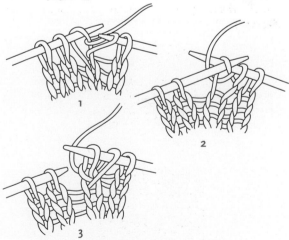

PURLWISE (P1F&B)

Work as for a knitwise bar increase, but purl into the front and back of the same stitch.

Lifted Increase

LEFT SLANT (LLI)

Insert left needle tip into the back of the stitch below the stitch just knitted (Figure 1), then knit this stitch through the back loop (Figure 2).

1   2

RIGHT SLANT (LRI)

Knit into the back of the stitch (in the "purl bump") in the row directly below the stitch on the needle (Figure 1), then knit the stitch on the needle (Figure 2), and slip the original stitch off the needle.

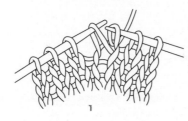

1   2

Make-One (M1) Increase

Note: Use the left slant if no direction of slant is specified.

LEFT SLANT (M1L)

With left needle tip, lift the strand between the last knitted stitch and the first stitch on the left needle from front to back (Figure 1), then knit the lifted loop through the back (Figure 2).

1   2

RIGHT SLANT (M1R)

With left needle tip, lift the strand between the needles from back to front (Figure 1). Knit the lifted loop through the front (Figure 2).

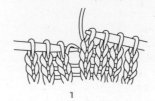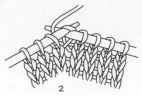

1   2

PICK UP AND KNIT

Along CO or BO Edge

With right side facing and working from right to left, insert the tip of the needle into the center of the stitch below the bind-off or cast-on edge (Figure 1), wrap yarn around needle, and pull through a loop (Figure 2). Pick up one stitch for every existing stitch.

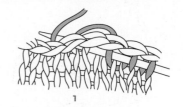

1

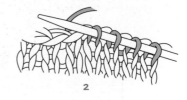

2

Along Selvedge Edge

With right side facing and working from right to left, insert tip of needle between last and second-to-last stitches, wrap yarn around needle, and pull through a loop. Pick up and knit about three stitches for every four rows, adjusting as necessary so that picked-up edge lays flat.

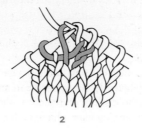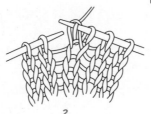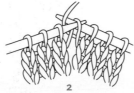

seams

Backstitch Seam—Horizontal

Pin pieces to be seamed with right sides facing together. Working from right to left into the stitch just below the bind-off row, bring threaded needle up between the second two stitches on each piece of knitted fabric, then back down through both layers, one stitch to the right of the starting point (**Figure 1**). *Bring the needle up through both layers one stitch to the left of the backstitch just made (**Figure 2**), then back down to the right, through the same hole used before (**Figure 3**). Repeat from *, working backward one stitch for every two stitches worked forward.

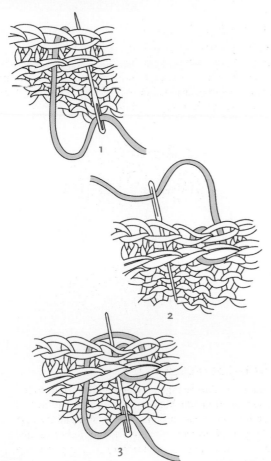

Grafting

HORIZONTAL GRAFTING

Working with the bound-off edges opposite each other, right sides of the knitting facing you, and working into the stitches just below the bound-off edges, bring threaded tapestry needle out at the center of the first stitch (i.e., go under half of the first stitch) on one side of the seam, then bring needle in and out under the first whole stitch on the other side (**Figure 1**). *Bring needle into the center of the same stitch it came out of before, then out in the center of the adjacent stitch (**Figure 2**). Bring needle in and out under the next whole stitch on the other side (**Figure 3**). Repeat from *, ending with a half-stitch on the first side.

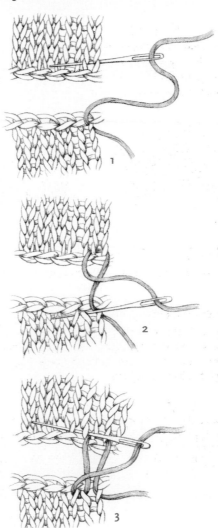

KITCHENER STITCH

Arrange stitches on two needles so that there is an equal number of stitches on each needle. Hold the needles parallel to each other with wrong sides of the knitting together. Allowing about ½" (1.3 cm) per stitch to be grafted, thread matching yarn on a tapestry needle. Work from right to left as follows:

Step 1. Bring tapestry needle through the first stitch on the front needle as if to purl and leave the stitch on the needle (**Figure 1**).

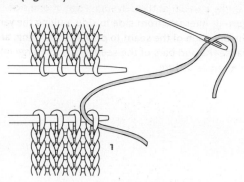

Step 2. Bring tapestry needle through the first stitch on the back needle as if to knit and leave that stitch on the needle (**Figure 2**).

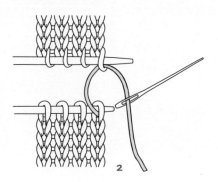

Step 3. Bring tapestry needle through the first front stitch as if to knit and slip this stitch off the needle. Then bring tapestry needle through the next front stitch as if to purl and leave this stitch on the needle (**Figure 3**).

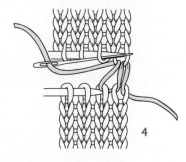

Step 4. Bring tapestry needle through the first back stitch as if to purl and slip this stitch off the needle. Then bring tapestry needle through the next back stitch as if to knit and leave this stitch on the needle (**Figure 4**).

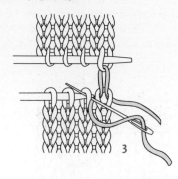

Repeat Steps 3 and 4 until one stitch remains on each needle, adjusting the tension to match the rest of the knitting as you go. To finish, bring tapestry needle through the front stitch as if to knit and slip this stitch off the needle. Then bring tapestry needle through the back stitch as if to purl and slip this stitch off the needle.

VERTICAL-TO-HORIZONTAL GRAFTING

*Bring threaded tapestry needle from back to front in the V of a knit stitch just below the bound-off edge. Insert the needle under one or two bars between the first and second stitch in from the selvedge edge on the adjacent piece, then back to the front of the same knit stitch just under the bound-off edge. Repeat from *, striving to match the tension of the knitting.

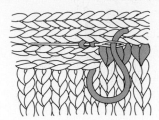

Mattress Stitch

Place the pieces to be seamed on a table, right sides facing up. Begin at the lower edge and work upward as follows for your stitch pattern:

SEED ST

For best results, use the tail from the cast-on row to start the seam and align lower edges. Then, with right sides facing you, beginning at the lower edge and working upward, insert threaded tapestry needle under the purl bar at the selvedge edge of one side **(Figure 1)**. Alternate from side to side, pulling the yarn in the direction of the seam to prevent stretching, and to cause the purl bars of the seed stitch to merge into a continuous texture.

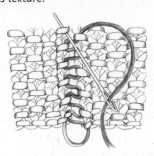

STOCKINETTE STITCH WITH 1-STITCH SEAM ALLOWANCE

Insert threaded needle under one bar between the two edge stitches on one piece, then under the corresponding bar plus the bar above it on the other piece (**Figure 1**). *Pick up the next two bars on the first piece (**Figure 2**), then the next two bars on the other (**Figure 3**). Repeat from *, ending by picking up the last bar or pair of bars on the first piece.

Slip-Stitch Crochet

To begin, place a slipknot on a crochet hook. With wrong side facing together and working one stitch at a time, *insert crochet hook through both thicknesses into the edge stitches (**Figure 1**), grab a loop of yarn and draw this loop through both thicknesses, then through the loop on the hook (**Figure 2**).

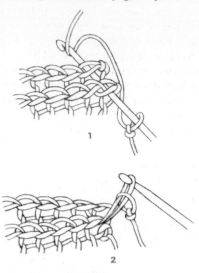

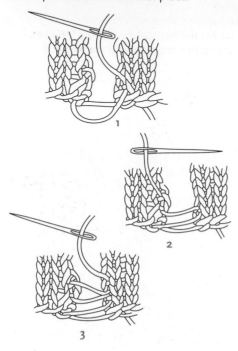

STOCKINETTE STITCH WITH ½-STITCH SEAM ALLOWANCE

To reduce bulk in the mattress stitch seam, work as for the 1-stitch seam allowance but pick up the bars in the center of the edge stitches instead of between the last two stitches.

Whipstitch

Hold pieces to be sewn together so that the edges to be seamed are even with each other. With yarn threaded on a tapestry needle, *insert needle through both layers from back to front, then bring needle to back in a spiral. Repeat from *, keeping even tension on the seaming yarn.

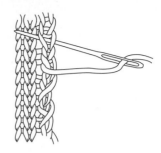

SHORT-ROWS

Knit Side

Work to turning point, slip next stitch purlwise (**Figure 1**), bring the yarn to the front, then slip the same stitch back to the left needle (**Figure 2**). Turn the work over and bring the yarn in position for the next stitch—one stitch has been wrapped and the yarn is correctly positioned to work the next stitch. When you come to a wrapped stitch on a subsequent row, hide the wrap by working it together with the wrapped stitch as follows: Insert right needle tip under the wrap (from the front if wrapped stitch is a knit stitch; from the back if wrapped stitch is a purl stitch; **Figure 3**), then into the stitch on the needle, and work the stitch and its wrap together as a single stitch.

Purl Side

Work to the turning point. Slip the next stitch purlwise to the right needle, bring the yarn to the back of the work (**Figure 1**), return the slipped stitch to the left needle, bring the yarn to the front between the needles (**Figure 2**), and turn the work so that the knit side is facing—one stitch has been wrapped and the yarn is correctly positioned to knit the next stitch. To hide the wrap on a subsequent purl row, work to the wrapped stitch, use the tip of the right needle to pick up the wrap from the back, place it on the left needle (**Figure 3**), then purl it together with the wrapped stitch.

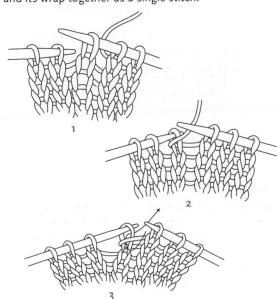

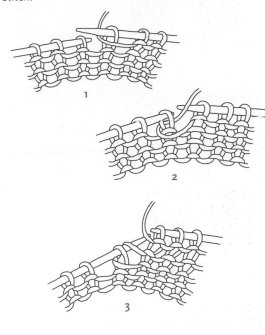

sources for yarn

Blue Heron Yarns
29532 Canvasback Dr., Ste #8
Easton, Maryland 21601
blueheronyarns.com

Cascade Yarns
PO Box 58168
1224 Andover Park East
Tukwila, WA 98188
cascadeyarns.com

Classic Elite Yarns
16 Esquire Rd., Unit 2
North Billerica, MA 01862
classiceliteyarns.com

Diamond Yarn
9697 Boul. St. Laurent, Ste.101
Montreal, QC
Canada H3L 2N1
and
155 Martin Ross Ave., Unit 3
Toronto, ON
Canada M3J 2L9
diamondyarn.com

Louet North America
3425 Hands Rd.
Prescott, ON
Canada K0E 1T0

Misti Alpaca
PO Box 2532
Glen Ellyn, Illinois 60138
mistialpaca.com

Patons
320 Livingstone Ave. S.
Box 40
Listowel, ON
Canada N4W 3H3

Plymouth Yarn Company, Inc.
500 Lafayette St.
Bristol, PA 19007
plymouthyarn.com

Westminster Fibers/Rowan Yarns
165 Ledge St.
Nashua, NY 03060
westminsterfibers.com
in Canada:
10 Roybridge Gate, Ste 200
Vaughan, Ontario L4H 3MB

Skacel Collection, Inc.
PO Box 88110
Seattle, WA 98138
skacelknitting.com

South West Trading Company
918 S. Park Ln., Ste. 102
Tempe, Arizona 85281
soysilk.com

Tahki-Stacy Charles Inc./Filatura di Crosa
70-60 83rd St., Bldg. #12
Glendale, NY 11385
tahkistacycharles.com
in Canada: Diamond Yarn

index

continue your knitting journey

with more inspiring resources from Vicki Square and Interweave

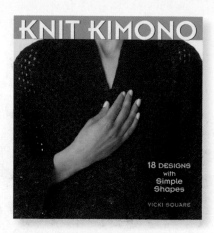

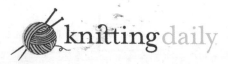
HILLSBORO PUBLIC LIBRARIES
Hillsboro, OR
Member of Washington County
COOPERATIVE LIBRARY SERVICES